All-Pro Recipes

Great "Chefs" of the NFL

MASTERS PRESS

A Division of Howard W. Sams
A Bell Atlantic Company

Published by Masters Press
(A Division of Howard W. Sams, a Bell Atlantic Company)
2647 Waterfront Pkwy E. Dr, Suite 300, Indianapolis, IN 46214

Published 1995

Printed in the United States of America

10 9 8 7 6 5 4 3 2

Library of Congress Cataloging-in-Publication Data

All-pro recipes / [by] great "chefs" of the NFL.
       p.   cm.
   ISBN 1-57028-058-4
    1. National Football League. 2. Cookery, American. 3. Football players -- United States.

TX715..A4242 1995   95-41121
641.5--dc20   CIP

Table of Contents

Our expert in the kitchen, Leo Moscato

Behind the Kitchens of the Pros

Paul Sheehy and Warren Schmidt

The recipes submitted in *All-Pro Recipes* were compiled primarily by Paul Sheehy and Warren Schmidt of Athlete Financial Management Service. Athlete Financial is a full service sports marketing and professional athlete representation firm based in Beverly Hills, California. Paul, an attorney, is the contract negotiator and has the bigger appetite. Warren heads up the marketing and public relations and is known to devour several dozen mozzarella sticks in a sitting. Together they compiled the recipes in this book over a four year period from their clients playing in the National Football League and from other current and former stars. This project was started as a fun diversion from the stress and high-stakes business of professional sports. And because they both always seemed to be hungry. A portion of the proceeds earned are being donated in each players' name to The Miami Project-Cure For Paralysis and other charitable and not-for-profit organizations.

Leo P. Moscato, Jr.

Leo is an executive chef and graduate of the world-renowned Culinary Institute of America in New York. Leo provided the culinary expertise to turn each recipe into an easy, fun and tasty dish, put together our collection of cooking tips in chapter six and served as the food stylist in all food photographs appearing in this book.

Marna Davis

Marna served as the marketing and publishing liason for Athlete Financial. Her creative input and enthusiastic attitude kept this project alive for so long.

Dedication

This book is dedicated to our families and friends, most of whom are huge football and foodlovers! We would specifically like to dedicate it to our mothers: Paulette Monaco; to Betty Ann Schmidt; to the memory of Angelina Moscato; and to the memory of Sharmon Davis.

Credits:
Interior artwork taken from Corel Clipart
Cover design by Phil Velikan
Front and back cover photos © Bob Shaw

Special Thanks

Bob Shaw of Powerhouse Productions in Dallas, Texas is responsible for the front and back cover photos.

Virgil Urbano for his time, effort and creative input in the compilation of these recipes.

Sipango! Restaurant in the Highland Park section of Dallas served as the backdrop for the cover shoot. This upscale restaurant and bar specializing in California Italian cuisine was the perfect host to some all-pro appetites and thirsts!

Susan Beard of Susan Beard Design in Philadelphia, Pennsylvania is responsible for the color food photographs which separate each chapter. Her assistants, Nash Rotter and Joe Castle III were also invaluable in the preparation and styling of the food shots. We would also like to thank Jeff Scholl for taking the photo of Chef Leo Moscato on page iv.

All player photographs appearing in this book are copyrighted material and were provided by, and with the express cooperation and permission of their respective National Football League teams.

Special thanks are due to the staff of Masters Press, especially Phil Velikan for coming up with the terrific design for the book's cover and Pat Brady, Terry Varvel and Heather Seal for their assistance with the book's layout and content.

Chef Leo would also like to thank Kathleen Coscia, Patricia Donnelly, Rick Tripodi, Pastor Michael Jude Fay and Henry "Bunny" Healey for their time and effort in helping him complete this project.

Metric Conversion Table
(For all of you CFL fans!)

To Change From	To	Multiply By
Ounces (oz.)	Grams (g)	28.35
Pounds (lbs.)	Kilograms (kg)	0.45
Teaspoons (tsp.)	Milliliters (ml)	5
Tablespoons (Tbsp.)	Milliliters (ml)	15
Fluid Ounces (oz.)	Milliliters (ml)	30
Cups (c)	Liters (l)	0.24
Pints (pt.)	Liters (l)	0.47
Quarts (qt.)	Liters (l)	0.95
Gallons (gal.)	Liters (l)	3.80
Temperature/Farenheit	Temperature/Celcius	subtract 32, then multiply by 5/9

Weights & Measure Equivalences
(It's third down and how long to go?)

Dash	less than 1/8 teaspoon
3 teaspoons	1 tablespoon or 1/2 fluid ounce
2 tablespoons	1/8 cup or 1 fluid ounce
4 tablespoons	1/4 cup or 2 fluid ounces
16 tablespoons	1 cup
1 gill	1/2 cup
1 cup	8 fluid ounces
2 cups	1 pint
2 pints	1 quart
4 quarts	1 gallon
8 quarts	1 peck
4 pecks	1 bushel
1 gram	.035 ounces
1 ounce	28.35 grams
16 ounces	1 pound or 453.59 grams
1 kilogram	2.21 pounds
1 lemon	1 to 1½ ounces of juice
1 orange	3 to 3½ ounces of juice
1 egg white	2 ounces for large egg

Game Day Nachos with Stuffed Portobellos

Appetizers

First Quarter
Scorecard

1

Jack Faulkner's Shrimp Spread

Roster

1 (8 oz.) package cream cheese
1 small can shrimp, cooked
1 tbsp. Worcestershire sauce
2 tbsp. lemon juice
2 tsp. minced onion
2 tsp. horseradish
Garlic salt to taste

Game Plan

1. Shred shrimp with a fork.
2. Combine all ingredients and refrigerate several hours.
3. Serve with crackers or French baguettes.

Serves 4-6

Jack T. Faulkner
St. Louis Rams

Jack has been involved in the NFL for over 40 years. He spent most of those years in the Rams front office involved in player, personnel and football operations. He also hosts an annual golf tournament to raise money for diabetes research.

Rodney Thomas
Houston Oilers

Rodney entered the NFL with the Miami Dolphins in 1988 and had a key 48 yard interception return against the Jets as a rookie. He spent three seasons with the Dolphins, then moved his show to the Rams and 49ers before landing in Houston for the 1995 season. Rodney is very active in youth services and gives freely of his time in this area.

Rodney Thomas' Classic Caesar Salad

Rodney credits his mother, Kader Thomas and grandmother Ella Stewart with this recipe!

Roster

2 good sized heads romaine lettuce
6-8 anchovy fillets
1 cup of virgin olive oil with roasted garlic flavor
Worcestershire sauce
2 hard boiled (10 minutes) eggs, peeled

1 lemon
6 oz. Parmesan cheese
Salt
½ tsp. dry mustard
Fresh ground pepper
2 small baguettes (loaves of French bread)

Game Plan

1. Slice the baguettes length-wise in ½ inch wide strips, brush on generous amounts of the flavored olive oil. Broil until golden brown, turning often. Set aside. These are your croutons.
2. Tear the lettuce into small, bite size pieces (do not cut with knife) and put them in a large salad bowl.
3. Sprinkle the dry mustard, pepper, anchovies and a splash of Worcestershire sauce over the lettuce. Salt to taste. Drizzle ½ cup of olive oil over the top.
4. Holding the eggs over the salad, crumble them and let them fall onto the top.
5. Squeeze the juice of an entire lemon all over the top of the salad.
6. Here's the key: Toss this salad very well. Be sure everything is well mixed. The better the toss, the better the salad!
7. Serve on individual plates with the bread strip croutons and sprinkle with the Parmesan cheese.

Serves 8

Suggestion: Make this a main course salad by adding shrimp or grilled chicken breast on the top!

Alphonso Taylor
San Diego Chargers

Alphonso is one of the largest players in the NFL, checking in at just over 350 pounds. He spent two seasons with the Cardinals and one with the Broncos before moving on to San Diego. He also played point guard for the Cardinals charity basketball team!

Alphonso Taylor's Tex-Mex Party Dip

Alphonso dipped into the recipe bag of Sallie Norris for this party favorite!

Roster

2 ripe avocados
2 tbsp. lemon juice
1 cup sour cream
1 pkg. taco seasoning
1 can of bean dip

1 tbsp. mayonnaise
1 cup chopped onions
2 diced tomatoes
1 small head of shredded lettuce
8 oz. sharp cheddar cheese

You will also need 3 small mixing bowls.

Game Plan

1. In bowl #1, mix the bean dip and the mayonnaise together
2. In bowl #2, mash the avocados and the lemon juice with a fork.
3. In bowl #3, mix the sour cream and the taco seasoning together.
4. In a large pie plate, neatly layer the mixes and remaining ingredients in the following order:
    bean dip & mayonnaise (bowl #1)
    avocado & lemon (bowl #2)
    sour cream & taco mix (bowl # 3)
    onion
    lettuce
    tomatoes
    cheese

Serves 8

Serve with Tortilla Chips! Always a hit!

Todd McNair's Southwestern Tortilla Wheel

Roster

3 extra large flour tortillas
½ cup of shredded yellow cheddar cheese
½ cup of shredded white cheddar cheese
1 large (30 oz.) can refried beans
½ cup sour cream

1 cup chopped green chilies (can is okay)
1 medium onion, diced
1 tsp. ground cumin
1 jar of ready-made salsa

Game Plan

1. Mix the refried beans, sour cream, onion, chilies and ground cumin in a bowl and let sit while preheating the oven to 425 degrees. Toss both cheeses together in a second bowl.
2. Put one tortilla in bottom of greased round casserole or baking dish and top with about ½ of the refried bean mix and ⅓ of the cheese.
3. Put a second tortilla on top and repeat step number 2.
4. Place the third tortilla on top and cover with remaining cheese.
5. Cover and bake at 425 for 20 minutes.
6. Garnish with a dollop of sour cream and salsa.
7. Cut in pie-shaped slices and serve!

Serves 8

Todd McNair
Houston Oilers

Todd has been a super kick and punt returner and clutch receiver out of the backfield during his career. He started out in 1988 with the Chiefs then joined the Oilers before the 1994 season.

Hamza Hewitt's Silver Dollar Pizzas

Roster

1 jar of pre-made tomato sauce
1 lb. loaf of bread dough (if frozen, be sure to thaw fully)
½ cup of shredded mozzarella cheese
¼ cup diced mushrooms
¼ cup diced pepperoni

Game Plan

1. Preheat oven to 425 degrees and grease a large baking sheet.
2. Slice dough into ½ inch thick slices and arrange with your fingers into small round pieces.
3. Place rounded dough on baking sheet about 3 inches apart.
4. Spoon sauce on each piece of dough and top with equal amounts of mushroom and pepperoni.
5. Top with mozzarella cheese.
6. Bake in oven at 425 degrees for 15 to 20 minutes or until crust appears brown.

Serves 4-6

Hamza Hewitt
Buffalo Bills

Hamza was originally drafted by the Cleveland Browns in 1994 and enjoyed an exciting season in Europe with the Scottish Claymores of the World League prior to signing with the Bills.

Roger Staubach
Dallas Cowboys

Known as Roger the Dodger for his scrambling heroics, Roger Staubach was a Heisman Trophy winning Navy midshipman before going on to lead the Cowboys to five Super Bowls between 1969 and 1979. He was named the MVP of Super Bowl VI against the Dolphins and was inducted to the Pro Football Hall of Fame in 1985.

Roger Staubach's Oriental Chicken Salad

Roger learned this recipe from a friend, Carol Chance.

Roster

8 (6 oz.) chicken breasts, grilled and cut into ½ inch strips
1 small onion — sliced
1 pkg. rice sticks — cooked and kept crisp
¼ cup toasted sesame seeds
1 tbsp. salt
1 head iceberg lettuce — torn
1 pkg. sliced toasted almonds

1 bunch chopped green onions, tops also
Dressing:
½ cup sugar
1 tsp. pepper
6-8 tbsp. sesame oil
2 tsp. salt
½ cup vinegar (apple cider is best)
1 cup vegetable oil

Game Plan

1. To prepare dressing: cook sugar, vinegar, salt and pepper until sugar dissolves. Let cool.
2. Add vegetable and sesame oil. Set aside.
3. Toss all salad ingredients just before serving, then add dressing.

Serves 6-8

Steve Largent
Seattle Seahawks

1995 will probably be remembered as Steve's most exciting year ever. He was elected to represent the state of Oklahoma in Congress and was inducted into the Pro Football Hall of Fame! During his career with the Seahawks, Steve was named to the Pro Bowl 7 times and he finished 2nd in NFL history in receptions (819), yards (13,089) and TD's (100).

Steve Largent's
Fruited Chicken Salad

Roster

4 cups diced cooked chicken—one roasted 3 lb. chicken is ideal for this recipe
2 cups seedless green grapes (or 15 oz. can pineapple chunks)
1 (11 oz.) can drained mandarin oranges
1 cup mayonnaise or favorite salad dressing

1 cup chopped celery
2 tbsp. grated onion or onion powder to taste
1 tbsp. prepared mustard
15 oz. can chow mein noodles
lettuce leaves for decoration

Game Plan

1. In a large bowl, combine chicken, grapes, celery, oranges and onion.
2. Blend in mayonnaise and mustard, toss gently with chicken mixture.
3. Cover and chill 2 hours.
4. Just before serving, mix in chow mein noodles and turn salad onto a lettuce lined bowl.

Serves 8

Daryl "Moose" Johnston
Dallas Cowboys

Greeted with a chorus of "Moooooose" each time he steps onto the field, Daryl has become a fan favorite in every NFL city. He has been selected to two Pro Bowls and has won two Super Bowls with the 'Boys. Daryl is pictured above with his sister.

Daryl Johnston's
Mushroom Sausage Croustades

Daryl learned this recipe from his mother, Ann Johnston.

Roster

18 slices white bread cut into 3-inch rounds
¼ cup butter
3 tsp. finely chopped shallots
½ lb. mushrooms, finely chopped
2 tbsp. flour
½ tsp. salt

1 ½ tbsp. chopped parsley
Ground red pepper
¼ lb. sweet Italian sausage
1 cup whipping cream
½ tsp. fresh lemon juice
2 tbsp. grated Parmesan cheese
1 ½ tbsp. chopped fresh chives

Game Plan

Croustades:

1. Preheat oven to 400 degrees
2. Butter small muffin tins.
3. Roll each bread round out to flatten and fit into muffin tins to form a cup.
4. Bake until lightly browned, about 8 minutes.
5. Remove from tin, let cool on rack.

Filling:

1. Sauté sausage, breaking up into small pieces until done. Remove and set aside.
2. Sauté shallots and mushrooms until liquid is evaporated.
3. Sprinkle with flour, chives, parsley, salt and pepper, and sausage.
4. Pour in cream and bring to a boil.
5. Reduce heat and simmer until mixture thickens.
6. Add lemon juice, let cool slightly.

Recipe is continued on the following page...

To Assemble:
1. Preheat oven to 350 degrees
2. Spoon filling evenly into croustades.
3. Set on baking sheet, sprinkle with cheese, and bake for 10 minutes.

Serves 8

Kitrick Taylor's Shrimp Toast

Roster

12 slices of white bread
1 lb. fresh shrimp
¼ cup finely chopped onion
1 ½ tsp. salt
1 tsp. sugar

1 tbsp. cornstarch
1 egg, beaten
1 (5 ¼ oz.) can water chestnuts, drained and finely chopped

Game Plan

1. Trim the crusts from the bread and discard the crusts. Dry bread in 300 degree oven for 5 minutes.
2. Chop shrimp very fine and mix with onion, salt, cornstarch and sugar.
3. Mix well. Add beaten egg and water chestnuts and mix again.
4. Spread mixture on bread and cut each slice into quarters, squares or triangles.
5. Heat oil about an inch deep and drop bread pieces, shrimp side down, into hot oil. Filling will not fall off.
6. Fry until edges of bread begin to brown, then turn on other side and fry until brown.

Serves 6-8

Kitrick Taylor
Denver Broncos

Kitrick's NFL career began with the Chiefs in 1988. He played for New England, Green Bay and San Diego before he made his way to the Broncos in 1993.

Mark Murphy
Green Bay Packers

Born in the birthplace of pro football, Canton, Ohio, Mark spent 12 years roaming the secondary with the Green Bay Packers. His reputation as a player is that of a fierce competitor and a very physical defensive back who brings the wood.

Murf's Hot Hot Wings

This is one of Mark's wife's favorite recipes!

Roster

8 to 10 lbs. of chicken wings
1 ½ sticks butter
16 oz. bottle Tabasco sauce
1 bottle favorite barbecue sauce (18 oz.)
1 bottle blue cheese salad dressing
1 bottle ranch salad dressing

Game Plan

1. Fry wings in deep fryer until crispy brown. Drain on paper towels.
2. In a large saucepan, heat Tabasco sauce, butter and barbecue sauce.
3. Place wings in sauce mixture and refrigerate overnight.
4. To heat, place wings under broiler until sizzling.

Enjoy with blue cheese and ranch dressing mixture.

Serves 8-10

Jon Hohman

Denver Broncos

Jon played linebacker for the Broncos during the team's AFL days from 1965 through 1967. He was one of the few bright spots on a team that won just a dozen games in those three seasons just prior to the NFL-AFL merger.

Hohman's Hot Fresh Mushroom Salad With Bubbly Garlic Bread

This is my favorite addition to an Italian meal!

Roster

Mushroom salad:
10 oz. spinach leaves, no stems
½ head romaine lettuce
½ lb. fresh mushrooms, cleaned and sliced

Dressing:
8 oz. bottle Italian vinagerette salad dressing
2 tsp. Dijon mustard
1 tsp. sugar

Garlic bread:
¼ cup melted butter or margarine
¼ cup grated Parmesan cheese
1 tsp. dried parsley flakes
½ tsp. garlic salt
1 egg, beaten
1 loaf frozen white bread dough

Game Plan

Salad:
1. Wash salad greens and break into bite size pieces. Add mushrooms and chill.
2. Mix dressing ingredients in microwave safe container, heat in microwave for three minutes or until hot.
3. Toss dressing with greens — serve immediately.

Garlic Bread:
1. Thaw 1 loaf of frozen white bread dough.
2. Mix butter, cheese, parsley, garlic salt and egg together.
3. Pinch off dough into 1½ to 2 inch size pieces.
4. Soak in above mixture for about 5 minutes.
5. Place in a lightly greased loaf pan.
6. Let rise and bake in 350 degree oven for about 30 minutes or until golden brown.

Serves 4

John Fina
Buffalo Bills

John was a first round draft choice of the Bills in 1992 and has been a fixture on the offensive line ever since. A native of Rochester, Minnesota, John played collegiately under the sun at the University of Arizona. One of his biggest thrills was catching a touchdown pass as an eligible receiver in a game in 1992 during his first of two Super Bowl seasons with the Bills.

John Fina's Artichoke Stuffed Portobello Mushrooms

Roster

2 portebello mushrooms	2 small jars artichoke hearts, halves
1 medium onion, diced small	1 medium Vidalia onion, diced small
6 slices fresh bread crumbs	1 tsp. thyme
15-20 green peppercorns	Pinch ground sage
2 tbsp. parsley	2 cups port wine
1 stick butter	Salt & pepper

Game Plan

1. Remove stems from mushrooms. Clean and dice the stems. Set the tops of the mushrooms aside.
2. Sauté onion until soft.
3. Chop one jar of the artichoke hearts; add this with the other jar and the diced mushroom stems to the onions in the pan.
4. Add thyme and sage. Let cool. Add salt and pepper to taste.
5. Add bread crumbs and parsley to artichokes and mix.
6. Place mushrooms in buttered baking dish stem side up.
7. Fill the two mushrooms with the stuffing, dividing the stuffing evenly.
8. Bake in 400 degree oven for 12 minutes.

Sauce:
Reduce port wine in small sauce pan with peppercorns, add butter and boil until thick. Pour over mushroom caps and serve.

Serves 2

Wesley Walker's
Game Day Nachos

This recipe is from Wesley's wife, Judy.

Roster

2 lb. ground beef
2 small cans tomato paste
1 can kidney beans
1 can black olives
5 hot green chili peppers
Nacho chips

2 pkg. Sloppy Joe seasoning
2 cups water
½ cup brown sugar
1 lb. sharp cheddar cheese
3 green onions

Game Plan

1. Brown ground beef, then add Sloppy Joe mix, tomato paste, and water. Mix well.
2. Add kidney beans and sugar. Mix again. Let simmer ½ hour.
3. While simmering, chop olives, peppers and onions, and shred cheese.
4. Arrange nacho chips on large platter and spoon on a generous helping of chili, then cheese, then sprinkle olives, peppers, and onions.
5. Microwave until cheese melts.
6. Dab spoonfuls of sour cream, salsa, and/or guacamole on top if desired.

Serve with margaritas or pina coladas — great while watching football — guaranteed to help you sleep through halftime!

Serves 8

Wesley Walker
New York Jets

Wesley lead the NFL in receiving yards in 1978 and he holds the Jets record for most touchdowns (4) and points (24) in a single game. One interesting thing about Wesley is that all of his accomplishments were earned despite the fact that he is legally blind in one eye.

Jeff Dellenbach's Taco Dip

Roster

1 can refried beans
1 can chilies
1 lb. ground beef
1 pkg. taco seasoning
1 can black olives, chopped
1 (12 oz.) pkg. cheddar cheese

1 (12 oz.) pkg. Monterey Jack cheese
1 large container sour cream
1 medium onion, chopped
2 large tomatoes, diced
Tortilla chips

Game Plan

1. Spread refried beans and chilies on bottom of 9x13" pan.
2. Brown ground beef with taco seasoning and layer on top of refried beans.
3. Layer black olives next.
4. Next, layer all cheese.
5. Bake at 350 degrees for 20 minutes.
6. Layer sour cream, diced onions and tomatoes on top.
7. Serve with warm tortilla chips.

Serves 8

Jeff Dellenbach
New England Patriots

Originally out of the University of Wisconsin, Jeff signed with the New England Patriots in 1995 after playing nine seasons with the Miami Dolphins. Jeff is one of the most consistent centers in the NFL and is relied upon to play guard in a pinch as well.

Bill Maas
Green Bay Packers

While Bill finished his career with the Packers, he played for nine seasons with the Kansas City Chiefs, including a pair of Pro Bowls. He is also the brother-in-law of record-setting quarterback Dan Marino of the Miami Dolphins.

Bill Maas' Crab Rangoon

Bill learned recipe from his friend Frankie.

Roster

1 lb. egg roll skins, cut in quarters
1 can crabmeat, finely chopped
¼ tsp. Worcestershire sauce
2 tsp. salt
Corn oil for deep frying

8 oz. cream cheese (room temp.)
1 clove garlic, chopped
3 drops Tabasco sauce
2 tsp. white pepper

Game Plan

1. Mix all ingredients except egg roll skins, beat vigorously until smooth and fluffy.
2. Put 1 tsp. crab mixture in center of each egg roll quarter. Moisten edges slightly.
3. Fold over into a triangle and close by pressing each side gently.
4. Deep fry in corn oil preheated 375 degrees until golden brown.

Serves 6-8

Serve with plum sauce with chopped scallions. Mmmmmmmmmmmm!

John Taylor
San Francisco 49ers

John is a two-time Pro-Bowl selection at wide receiver and has been a key contributor to the 49ers success over the last decade with over 5,000 career receiving yards. He was also the recipient of the 1992 United Way Professional Athlete Volunteer Award for Community Service.

Taylor's Italian Style Stuffed Clams

Compliments of Maria Esposito.

Roster

1 dozen large hard-shell clams, scrubbed (Quahogs)
½ bag frezelles (hard Italian pepper toast)
½ cup parsley, chopped
3 cloves garlic, minced
1 cup black olives, drained & chopped
½ cup olive oil

Game Plan

1. Steam clams in small amount of water until open. Save broth for next step.
2. Soak frezelles in clam broth until soft, then squeeze bread and place in mixing bowl.
3. Mix well with the remainder of the ingredients.
4. Remove clams from shells, separate each clam shell into two single shells.
5. Chop clam meat into small pieces. Use bellies if desired — they are optional for this recipe.
6. Mix clams with bread mixture and add olive oil. Mix well.
7. Oil each shell first, then stuff.
8. Bake on cookie sheet for about 30 minutes in 350 degree preheated oven until golden brown.

Makes 24 stuffed clams, which serves 12

This is an original Italian family recipe and is truly outstanding.

Neil Lomax
Phoenix Cardinals

Neil once threw seven TD passes in a single half while at Portland State. He holds the Cardinals' single season passing marks of 4,614 yards and 28 TD's, and the single game mark of 468 yards.

Eggs "Neil" Benedict

Roster

4 eggs, poached
1 tsp. butter
4 slices Canadian bacon
2 toasted English muffins
1 serving Hollandaise sauce
1 tsp. chives
¼ cup chopped green onions
4 thin slices cheese (your choice)

Game Plan

1. Toast English muffins.
2. Poach eggs in water (add a few drops of white vinegar so eggs keep whole).
3. Place Canadian bacon and cheese on muffins, broil for two minutes.
4. Sauté green onions and chives together for one minute in butter.
5. Place one egg on each muffin top with chives and onions.
6. Top each muffin with Hollandaise sauce*.

Serves 2

*Hollandaise sauce can be made quickly and easily from a package mix.

Cheddar Cheese & Kielbasa Soup

Soups & Stews

Second Quarter Scorecard

Dave Toub's Seafood Stew

This is a favorite with Dave's wife, Cheryl, and son, Shane.

Roster

1 (16 oz.) can stewed tomatoes
1 (10 ¾ oz.) can condensed tomato soup
1 (10¾ oz.) can condensed chicken gumbo soup
2 dozen well-scrubbed mussels
2 soup cans water (2 ½ cups)
1 medium sweet potato, chopped and peeled
1 stalk celery, chopped

⅓ cup chopped green onion
1 tbsp. chopped parsley
1 tbsp. Worcestershire sauce
1 clove garlic, minced
2 dashes Tobasco sauce
1 bay leaf
1 (7½ oz.) can clams
1 (4½ oz.) can shrimp
Salt & pepper

Game Plan

1. In a large saucepan, combine undrained stewed tomatoes, all canned soup, water, sweet potato, celery, onion, parsley, Worcestershire sauce, garlic, tobasco sauce and bay leaf.
2. Bring to a boil and reduce heat. Let simmer for 30 minutes or until vegetables are tender.
3. Add undrained clams and drained shrimp. Simmer 10 more minutes.
4. Steam mussels in about 3-4 inches of water separately. Strain 1 cup of broth and add to the stew along with the mussels just before serving.
5. Remove bay leaf and serve very hot.

Serves 6

Dave Toub
Philadelphia Eagles

Dave was drafted as a center by the Philadelphia Eagles in 1984 following a super college career at both UTEP and Springfield College. He is the head strength and conditioning coach for the University of Missouri.

Lester Holmes
Philadelphia Eagles

Lester was the Eagles' first round draft pick in 1993 and is expected to be a fixture at offensive guard for many years to come. Lester was born and raised in Tylertown, Mississippi and stayed at home to play college ball at Jackson State.

Lester Holmes'
Big Time Clam Chowder

Roster

2 tbsp. butter
1 medium onion, chopped
2 stalks celery, chopped
1 ½ tsp. granulated garlic or garlic powder
½ tsp. white pepper

Pinch thyme
2 tbsp. clam broth (use juice from clams)
¼ cup flour
6 cups clam juice
2 cups fresh chopped clams
2 medium potatoes, peeled & diced

Game Plan

1. Melt butter in saucepan, adding onion, celery, garlic, pepper and thyme. Cook over low heat until soft.
2. Whisk the clam broth and flour together. Add to the butter mixture, whisking everything together until smooth. Cook 5 minutes.
3. In a separate pot, heat the clam juice and clams, then add the onion-celery mixture and cook 15 minutes.
4. Add the potatoes last and cook until they are tender.

Serves 8

Makes 2 quarts.

John Offerdahl
Miami Dolphins

John broke into the NFL in a big way — he was named to the Pro Bowl as a rookie and 4 times more after that! He is very active in the Miami community and has recently opened a bagel shop!

John Offerdahl's Christmas Oyster Stew

This recipe comes from John's mother and her family.

Roster

4 tbsp. flour
4 tbsp. water
1 tsp. salt
Dash pepper
1 qt. fresh shucked oysters

2 qt. whole milk
1 cup light cream
Paprika
Butter

Game Plan

1. Combine the flour, water, salt and pepper and blend into a smooth paste.
2. Stir mixture into oysters and oyster liquid.
3. Simmer over very low heat until edges of oysters curl.
4. Pour in scalded milk while hot and cream.
5. Remove pot from heat and cover, let stand 15 minutes to improve taste.
6. At serving time, place one pat of butter and sprinkle paprika on top of each serving.
7. Serve with oyster crackers.

Serves 8

An old family recipe and a Christmas tradition in our house.

Lombardi's Zuppa di Pesce

Roster

3 lb. assorted sliced fish
1½ tsp. salt
½ tsp. crushed bay leaf
1 clove garlic, minced
1 cup dry white wine
12 small hard-shell clams

⅓ cup olive oil
½ tsp. pepper
1 cup chopped onions
2 tbsp. tomato paste
2 cups boiling water

Game Plan

1. Cut fish into small 3-4" pieces.
2. Heat olive oil in large saucepan, brown fish lightly and add salt, pepper, and bay leaf. Cook on low for about 10 minutes, turning fish once.
3. Remove fish carefully and set aside.
4. In the oil remaining, sauté the onions for 10-12 minutes, then add garlic, tomato paste, and wine. Then add the boiling water.
5. Add scrubbed clams and cook on medium for about 20 minutes. Discard any clams that don't open.
6. Add fish about 5 minutes before serving.
7. Taste for seasoning and serve in large bowls with Italian bread.

Serves 4-6

Michael Lombardi
Cleveland Browns

Mike is the Director of Player Personnel for the Browns and is one of the most respected front-office people in the NFL.

Tim Krumrie's Cheddar Cheese and Kielbasa Soup

Roster

1 onion, chopped
¼ cup butter
¾ tsp. dry mustard
2 cups chicken broth
2 potatoes, sliced
3 cups shredded cheddar cheese
½ lb. kielbasa

2 stalks celery, chopped
¼ cup flour
2 tsp. Worcestershire sauce
2 carrots, sliced
3 cups milk
¼ tsp. pepper

Game Plan

1. Sauté onion and celery in butter 3 minutes.
2. Stir in flour, mustard, and Worcestershire sauce. Cook and stir for 2 minutes.
3. Stir in broth, carrots, potatoes, and kielbasa. Bring to boiling, lower heat, cover.
4. Simmer, stirring for 25 minutes.
5. Add milk, cover, and cook over medium heat until almost boiling. Reduce heat to low and add cheese. Heat until cheese is melted.

Serves 4-6

Tim Krumrie
Cincinnati Bengals

Tim was a 10th round selection of the Bengals in 1983 out of Wisconsin and was voted to two Pro Bowls during his career. He is on the Board of Directors for the Wisconsin Committee for Prevention of Child Abuse and speaks at many schools on goals, motivation and overcoming adversity.

Buck Buchanan
Kansas City Chiefs

Buck played defensive tackle for the Chiefs from 1963 through 1975. During that time, Buck played in a pair of Super Bowls and earned a ring for a 23-7 win over the Vikings in Super Bowl IV. He was inducted into the Hall of Fame in 1990. This recipe was submitted in Buck's memory by his wife, Georgia. After his death in 1992, she has worked hard to continue the community work started by Buck. He was founder of the Special Olympics in Kansas and Missouri and he sponsored and organized an annual Sports Carnival to raise money for people with special needs.

Buck Buchanan's Gumbo

Roster

List #1:
5-7 lb. shrimp
1 large hen
1 lb. fresh crabmeat

1 (16 oz.) can tomatoes, cut up
1 can Italian or Creole sauce
2 pkg. cut-up okra
1 box crab & shrimp mix

List #2:
Chicken fat or bacon drippings
1 stalk celery
1 bunch green onions, chopped
3 green peppers, chopped
1 can tomato sauce
1 can mushrooms, sliced pieces
1 can water chestnuts, diced
4 onions, chopped
3 garlic pods

Dashes of:
Russian salad dressing
Paprika
Tabasco sauce
Chili powder
Worcestershire sauce
Dry mustard
Cayenne
A few bay leaves

Game Plan

1. Cover hen with water, add a tablespoon each of the green peppers, onions, celery, and bay leaves. Boil until tender, let cool, save stock. Be sure not to overcook. Pieces should be firm, not stringy. Cut chicken into small chunks, let marinate in stock.
2. Creole sauce: Sauté the remainder of the first five ingredients from list 2 in chicken fat or bacon drippings. Mix together tomatoes, sauces, some chicken stock and dashes of the other seasonings, along with the bag of crab-shrimp boil mix.
3. Make a roux with flour and chicken stock (whisk together) and stir into mixture. Cook and stir until it thickens.
4. Cook shrimp in chicken stock until pink, then combine with chicken and Creole sauce. Add okra, mushrooms, water chestnuts and crabmeat. DO NOT OVERCOOK. Serve over fluffy rice.

Serves 6

Rocky Bleier
Pittsburgh Steelers

Rocky was a key part of the Steelers dynasty of the 1970s and a fan favorite. A Vietnam veteran, Rocky captured the hearts of Americans with his never-say-die attitude.

Rocky's Meatless Chili

Roster

1 lb. pinto beans
6 cloves garlic
1/3 cup chili powder
1/2 tsp. red cayenne pepper
1 can (28 oz.) chopped tomatoes, drained
10 oz. frozen corn
3/4 cup chopped black olives

2 large onions
3 tbsp. vegetable oil
1 tbsp. cumin
7-9 cups chicken broth
1 red pepper chopped small
3/4 cup bulgur wheat
2 tbsp. Worcestershire sauce

Game Plan

1. Sauté oil, onion, garlic, add chili powder, cayenne pepper, cumin. Cook 30 minutes.
2. Add beans and water (just enough to cover). Simmer 45 minutes to 1 hour.
3. Add chicken broth, tomatoes, red pepper, and corn — simmer 20 minutes.
4. Stir in remaining garlic, olives, and Worcestershire sauce — simmer 5 more minutes.

Serves 4-6

In this world of health consciousness, this is a wonderful recipe to satisfy all those chili lovers without the fat and calorie content of the more traditional chili recipes.

Rathman's Carbonnade à la Flamande (Beef in Beer Stew)

An old Rathman family recipe.

Roster

3 lb. chuck beef cut into 2 inch cubes
3 tbsp. flour
8 oz. canned beef broth
1 tsp. vinegar
1 tsp. thyme
4 tbsp. butter

1 large onion
16 oz. beer
1 tsp. garlic, chopped
1 tsp. sugar
1 tsp. salt

Game Plan

1. Preheat oven to 300 degrees.
2. Sear beef in hot skillet, remove meat to casserole dish but save juice in pan.
3. Add onions to juice in pan and brown slightly. Remove onions and set aside with meat.
4. Add butter to remaining juice in pan then add flour, stirring constantly.
5. Pour beer and broth into pan, bring to a boil, stirring constantly.
6. Add remaining spices and pour over meat.
7. Cover casserole tightly, cook for 2 hours.

Serves 8-10

Tom Rathman
Oakland Raiders

Tom is the prototype true fullback in the NFL. Known for his tough inside running, hard hitting blocks and soft hands, Tom spent years with the 49ers before wearing the Silver and Black.

Chef Leo's Famous French Onion Soup

Roster

3 medium onions, cut in half and sliced
2 cups chicken broth
2 cups beef broth
1 tbsp. brown sugar
2 tbsp. vegetable oil
1 tsp. thyme
1 tsp. oregano
2 cloves, whole

1 bay leaf
Salt and pepper to taste

Optional:
2 oz. sherry wine
4 large croutons
4 slices swiss cheese

Game Plan

1. Place oil and onions in a frying pan over medium heat.
2. Cook onions until carmelized* (dark golden brown).
3. Add chicken and beef broth, thyme, oregano, cloves, bay leaf and brown sugar.
4. Let simmer 30 minutes, add salt and pepper to taste.

Optional:
— Before serving add sherry wine.
— For a classical treat, place soup in ovenproof crocks, place a crouton on top of the soup, then top with cheese and bake in 400 degree oven for 5-10 minutes.

*Carmelization is when you cook a food product slowly until the sugar content is released to create the sweet flavor and dark golden brown appearance of the product.

Third Quarter

Stuffed Olives

Side Dishes

Third Quarter
Scorecard

Pat Hegarty's Spinach Casserole

John and Annette Passander gave Pat the secrets to this recipe!

Roster

2 pkg. frozen chopped spinach, rinsed and drained
1 can Durkee™ french fried onions
½ cup water
2 hard boiled eggs, chopped small
2 cups unflavored bread crumbs
Garlic salt
1 can cream of mushroom soup
4 oz. can drained mushrooms
1 small pkg. Velveeta™ cheese, diced
1 stick melted butter

Game Plan

1. Preheat oven to 350 degrees.
2. Blend all ingredients except butter, garlic salt, bread crumbs, and onions.
3. Sprinkle flat baking dish with garlic salt then add spinach mixture.
4. Top with garlic salt, french fried onions and buttered crumbs.
5. Bake for about 40 minutes, or until bubbly.

Serves 4-6

Pat Hegarty
Denver Broncos

Pat was an academic all-American coming out of UTEP and he spent two seasons as a backup with the Denver Broncos, including one trip to the Super Bowl.

Marvin Goodwin
Philadelphia Eagles

Marvin was drafted by the Eagles out of UCLA and is a steady performer on both special teams and in the secondary.

Marvin Goodwin's Home Style Corn Fritters

Roster

1 lb. can of whole kernel corn or 2 cups fresh kernels, drained
2 eggs, separated
¼ tsp. salt
3 tbsp. milk
2 tbsp. flour
1 tsp. sugar

Game Plan

1. Mix corn, egg yolks, milk, flour, salt and sugar in a bowl.
2. Beat egg whites separately until stiff and fold into batter.
3. Drop batter by spoonful into hot oil in frying pan, cook until done, turning once.

Serves 4

Great with hot syrup or butter...very easy and very good!

Grandma Hillman's Mustard Pickles

These are excellent on hot dogs and sausage!

Roster

6 large cucumbers	3 tbsp. flour
¼ cup salt	1 tbsp. mustard
1 quart onions	1 tbsp. turmeric
1 pint vinegar	1 tsp. mustard seed
2 cups sugar	1 tsp. celery seed

Game Plan

1. Peel cucumbers and remove seeds.
2. Cut very fine as for relish.
3. Add salt and let stand overnight.
4. Drain in the morning and add finely chopped onions and remaining ingredients.
5. Cook for 1 hour and bottle.

Serves 6-8

Jay Hillman
San Francisco 49ers

Jay rushed for over 2,000 yards during his career at Boston University and has played in the NFL for both the Cowboys and 49ers. While in minicamp with the 49ers, Jay served as an extra in Eddie Murphy's movie Beverly Hills Cop II.

Cherry's Chili Rice

Roster

1 lb. ground beef
1 pkg. chili seasoning mix
¼ cup chopped onions
¼ cup chopped bell peppers
1 tsp. oregano
½ to ¾ lb. hot sausage

23 oz. red kidney beans
15 oz. can stewed tomatoes
1 tsp. parsley
Touch of black pepper
Touch of Tabasco
2 cups cooked rice

Game Plan

1. Brown and drain ground beef.
2. Brown and drain sausages.
3. Mix chili seasoning with beans, mix in onions, peppers and stewed tomatoes.
4. Bring to a boil, then turn down and simmer until beans are soft, about 30-35 minutes,
5. Add parsley and oregano, blend in a touch of Tabasco and black pepper.
6. Serve over rice, with crackers on the side.

Raphel Cherry
Detroit Lions

Raphel played his first years in pro football with the Washington Redskins prior to joining the Lions. Raphel was known as a key special teams performer and a ball-hawking defensive back during his career in the NFL.

Dale Hellestrae
Dallas Cowboys

Dale was with the Buffalo Bills and Los Angeles Raiders before joining the Cowboys. At 6'7" he is one of the tallest centers in the NFL...and the owner of a pair of Super Bowl rings.

Dale Hellestrae's Zucchini Cream Cheese Pancakes

Learned recipe from Mom

Roster

5 medium size zucchini, shredded very finely
¼ cup parmesan cheese
½ tsp. garlic powder
¼ tsp. pepper

3 eggs
½ cup flour
½ tsp. salt
3 oz. cream cheese

Game Plan

1. Mix all ingredients together thoroughly.
2. Heat skillet on medium heat and coat with vegetable cooking spray.
3. Drop batter (6 oz. ladle) into skillet, brown on both sides.

Serves 6

These are very delicious and are always a big hit. They can be buttered and sprinkled with Parmesan cheese or can be served plain.

Troy Aikman
Dallas Cowboys

Considered the premier QB in the NFL, Troy is a four-time Pro Bowl selection, two-time Super Bowl winner and a Super Bowl MVP. Troy established the Troy Aikman Foundation in 1992 to aid children's charities in the Dallas area.

Aikman's Famous Potatoes and Eggs with Cheese

Roster

4 potatoes (1½ cups), no need to peel
⅓ cup finely chopped onions
1 cup sour cream
1 tbsp. butter
3 tbsp. flour
1 cup sharp cheddar cheese, shredded
2 tbsp. snipped parsley

1 tsp. pepper
1 cup soft bread crumbs
2 tbsp. paprika
½ cup milk or half & half
4 hard-boiled eggs, sliced
2 tbsp. melted butter

Game Plan

1. Boil whole potatoes in salted water until soft, but centers are firm. Drain and slice
2. Sauté onion in butter until tender, then blend in flour, sour cream, cheese, milk, parsley, salt and pepper.
3. Continue cooking over low heat until cheese melts.
4. Combine this mixture with sliced potatoes.
5. Layer half the potato mixture in a casserole dish and arrange egg slices over potatoes.
6. Sprinkle with salt and pepper.
7. Top with remaining potato mixture and toss bread crumbs with melted butter and paprika, sprinkle over casserole.
8. Bake at 350 degrees for about 45 minutes.

Serves 8

Shack's Yummy Yams

Roster

3 large yams
1 cup brown sugar
1 tbsp. cinnamon
2 sticks butter
2 tbsp. vanilla
1 tbsp. nutmeg

Game Plan

1. Peel yams and slice into medium size wedges, boil for 30 minutes.
2. Drain and place cooked yams in large flat baking dish.
3. Place pats of butter on top of yams, then sprinkle with brown sugar, spices and vanilla.
4. Do not stir.
5. Bake for 55 minutes in preheated 400 degrees oven.

Serves 5-10

My life long love of southern cooking inspired this down home recipe.

James "Shack" Harris
L.A. Rams

James led the NFC in passing in 1976 and in 1975 he was the Most Valuable Player of the Pro Bowl. During his career with the Rams, James lead the team to a pair of NFC West titles and took the team to two conference championship games. He finished his career backing up Hall of Famer Dan Fouts as a member of the San Diego Chargers following a 1977 trade.

John Cappelletti's Stuffed Olives Supreme

Roster

1 lb. ground meat
2 eggs
1 tsp. grated cheese
1 lb. large green Spanish olives

1 cup bread crumbs
1 clove garlic, minced
2 eggs-well beaten
Parsley and pepper to taste (no salt)

Game Plan

1. In a large mixing bowl, thoroughly blend ground meat, eggs, bread crumbs, parsley, pepper, grated cheese and minced garlic.
2. Stuff pitted olives with ground meat mixture.
3. Coat each olive with beaten eggs, then roll in flour.
4. Fry in oil until browned. Remove from heat and drain on paper towel.
5. Serve immediately.

Serves 6-8

John Cappelletti
L.A. Rams

John won the Heisman Trophy as a star running back at Penn State in 1973 before continuing on to a successful NFL career with the Rams. He is perhaps best known for the most gracious and famous Heisman Award acceptance speech of all time, as he gave the award to his brother, Joey, who was terminally ill.

Bobby Bell
Kansas City Chiefs

Bobby was enshrined in the Pro Football Hall of Fame in 1983 following an 11 year career at linebacker for the Chiefs from 1963-1974. He returned 6 interceptions for touchdowns during his career.

Bobby Bell's Sweet Potato Pie

Roster

4 medium sweet potatoes
1 1/2 cup sugar
1 14 oz. can of condensed milk
4 eggs
1 ready made pie shell, baked for 10 minutes at 400 degrees

½ tsp. cinnamon
2 sticks softened butter
2 tsp. vanilla
½ tsp. nutmeg

Game Plan

1. Preheat oven to 400 degrees.
2. Boil whole potatoes in jackets until tender, then run under cool water and peel.
3. Mash potatoes, then blend in all other ingredients with electric mixer.
4. Pour mixture into pie shells, and bake at 400 degrees for 10 minutes.
5. Reduce heat to 350 degrees and bake 40-45 minutes longer, until set.
6. Cool and serve.

Serves 6-8

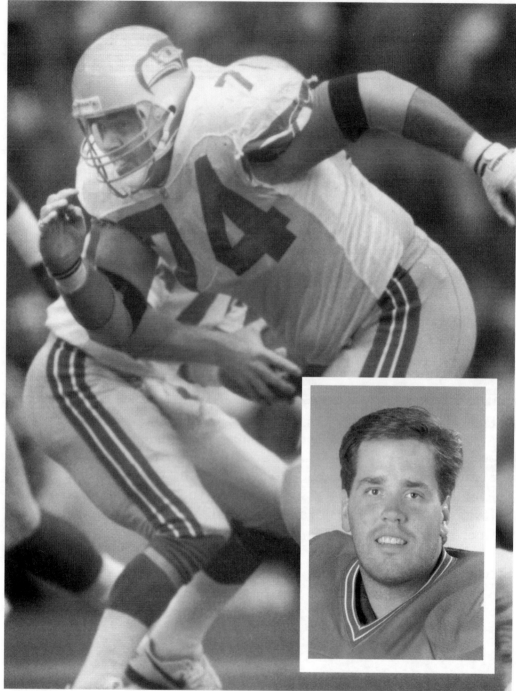

Warren Wheat
Seattle Seahawks

Warren is a big lineman from BYU who began his career with the Rams before joining the Seahawks in 1989.

Wheat's Onion Broccoli Deluxe

This recipe came from Warren's Mom.

Roster

1 pkg. (10 oz.) frozen cut broccoli
1 cup diced onion
3 oz. pkg. cream cheese
¼ cup parmesan cheese
2 tbsp. flour

4 tbsp. butter
1 cup milk
1 cup bread crumbs
Dash of salt and pepper

Game Plan

1. Preheat oven to 350 degrees.
2. Cook broccoli according to directions, along with the onions. Drain.
3. In saucepan, blend flour, salt and pepper with 2 tbsp. butter. Cook and stir until bubbly.
4. Blend in cream cheese until smooth, then stir in cooked vegetables.
5. Melt remaining butter and toss with bread crumbs and cheese. Pour over casserole.
6. Bake 15-20 minutes.

Serves 4-6

Hershel Walker
New York Giants

This former Heisman Trophy winner was traded by the Cowboys to the Vikings for 6 players and 12 draft picks! The most ever traded for one player! He later went on to play for the Eagles before landing in New York for the 1995 season. He is pictured above with his wife.

Hershel Walker's Potato Casserole

Roster

6 cooked potatoes
¼ cup butter, melted
1 tsp. salt
2 cups sour cream — room temperature
2 cups cheddar cheese
⅓ cup green onion, chopped
¼ tsp. pepper
3 tbsp. butter

Game Plan

1. Preheat oven to 300 degrees.
2. Peel cooked potatoes and coarsely shred them.
3. Add cheese and melted butter, mix lightly.
4. Add onion, salt, pepper, and sour cream.
5. Mix lightly, place in casserole dish and dot with butter.
6. Bake for 25 minutes.

Serves 8

Chuck Bednarik
Philadelphia Eagles

Chuck was known as one of the fiercest linebackers ever to play the game. Inducted into the Hall of Fame in 1967, Chuck dominated the NFL at his position from 1949 through 1962.

Bednarik's Cabbage Rolls

Roster

3 lb. each of beef, pork and veal
2 cups onions, diced
32 oz. draned saurkraut
3 8 oz. cans tomato soup
1 smoked ham hock
1 tbsp. salt and pepper

1½-2 cups cooked rice, cool
4 large heads cabbage
1 tbsp. seasoned salt
2 cloves garlic minced
2 tbsp. butter

Game Plan

1. Remove core from cabbage.
2. Boil whole cabbage and remove leaves as they become wilted and save wilted leaves.
3. Sauté chopped onion in butter until transparent.
4. Add onions to meat with rice, salt, pepper, seasoned salt and garlic, mix together thoroughly. Set aside.

To Stuff:
1. Fill each wilted cabbage leaf with a tablespoon of the meat mixture, roll up and tuck in ends.
2. Place remaining cabbage leaves on bottom of a large deep pot.
3. Place saurkraut rolls on cabbage and half of tomato soup over rolls.
4. Fill pot with water up to cover first layer of rolls.
5. Fill pot with more rolls, ham hock and the remainder of the soup.
6. Bring to a boil and simmer 1 ½ to 2 hours.
7. Save juice and serve as a soup.

Makes 100 rolls — freezes well.

Dave Krieg
Arizona Cardinals

Dave played for 11 seasons with the Seattle Seahawks. During that span he enjoyed a string of 28 straight games with a TD pass and was named to a trio of Pro Bowls. He also set the NFL record for most career fumbles with over 125. Dave joined the Cardinals after two seasons with the Chiefs and a very brief stint with the Lions.

Dave's Favorite Potato Dish

Roster

2 lb. hash browns
1 can cream of mushroom soup
½ onion, diced
1 pint sour cream
1 cup shredded cheddar cheese
½ cup melted butter

Game Plan

1. Preheat oven to 350 degrees.
2. Combine hash browns, mushroom soup, onion, sour cream and cheddar cheese.
3. Put mixture in 9x9" baking dish, top with cornflake crumbs mixed with butter.
4. Bake for one hour.

Serves 6-8

Baker's Best Habanero Beans & Onions

Roster

16 oz. Cooked white northern beans
1 large yellow onion — diced small
1 habanero pepper — diced small
1 garlic clove

1 cup chicken stock
1 tbsp. olive oil
1/4 tsp. salt
1 14" black iron pan

Game Plan

1. Sauté the onions and the habanero pepper in 1 tbsp. of olive oil in the iron pan until golden brown.
2. Add the garlic and beans and sauté until a crust forms at the bottom of the pan.
3. Add the salt and chicken stock, scraping the bottom of the pan with a wooden spoon.
4. Simmer for 10 minutes.
5. Add 1 tbsp. of olive oil and serve.

Serves 4

Jon Baker
Dallas Cowboys

Joe signed with the Dallas Cowboys as a free agent following a star-studded college career at Arizona State University. He was the only barefooted kicker to enter the 1995 NFL season (ouch!). Jon has established himself as the Cowboys' kickoff specialist, handling all kickoff duties due to his powerful leg which drives the ball deep and high.

Fourth Quarter

Cajun Shrimp Fettuccini

Entreés

Fourth Quarter Scorecard

Michael Brandon's Crab Pie

Roster

1½ cups crab meat
2 tbsp. flour
6 oz. grated cheddar cheese
Pinch of salt
1 small red pepper, diced
4 egg whites

⅓ cup diced onion
Old Bay seafood seasoning to taste
½ cup mayonnaise
1 nine-inch pie shell
½ cup milk

Game Plan

1. Preheat oven to 350 degrees.
2. Bake pie shell according to directions.
3. Mix all ingredients and pour into cooked pie shell.
4. Bake at 350 degrees for 35-40 minutes.

Serves 6

Serve warm or cold and refrigerate unused portion.

Michael Brandon
San Franciso 49ers

Michael terrorized quarterbacks all across the globe, as he was one of the top performers in the World League prior to signing with the 49ers. His career began with the Indianapolis Colts and he also spent time with the Miami Dolphins and Arizona Cardinals following a collegiate career with the Florida Gators.

Paul Siever's
Orzo Spinach Pilaf

Roster

6 oz. orzo pasta
1 tbsp. plus 1 tsp. olive oil
1 cup chopped onion
1 cup chopped celery
2 garlic cloves, minced
½ cup low-sodium chicken broth

1 tbsp. red wine vinegar
3 oz. shredded Monterey Jack cheese
Black pepper to taste
2 cups thawed frozen chopped spinach,
squeezed dry

Game Plan

1. Cook and drain orzo.
2. In a skillet, heat oil, add onions, celery and garlic. Cook until tender.
3. Stir in spinach, half the chicken broth, and vinegar.
4. Cook 2-3 minutes, until liquid evaporates.
5. Add orzos, cheese and the rest of the chicken broth. Stir mixture, cook for two more minutes.
6. Sprinkle with pepper and serve.

Serves 8

Paul Siever
Jacksonville Jaguars

Paul was one of the first players ever signed by the Jaguars. Before the Jags, Paul played offensive guard with the Redskins and Bears.

Brian O'Neal's Shrimp with Rice and Cheese

Roster

1 lb. unpeeled shrimp
1 cup white wine (or more)
4 fresh tomatoes
3 cloves garlic
1 medium onion
3-4 tbsp. olive oil

¼ cup chopped fresh parsley
1 cup brown rice
1 tsp. tomato paste
Freshly ground salt & pepper
2 tbsp. Parmesan cheese

Game Plan

1. Peel the shrimp, leaving a few unpeeled for garnish.
2. Add the shells to the wine and bring to a boil. Allow mixture to cool completely before removing shells from wine. Strain.
3. Peel and chop tomatoes, garlic and onion. Set tomatoes aside.
4. Sauté the garlic and onion in olive oil without browning them.
5. Stir in parsley then add the uncooked rice. Mix well.
6. Add the wine, tomato paste and tomatoes and just enough water to cover the rice.
7. Season with salt & pepper and cook for 20-30 minutes, until rice is done.
8. After the rice is cooked, stir in the shrimp and cheese. Heat through again.
9. Garnish with unpeeled shrimp and a sliced lemon and serve.

Serves 4

Brian O'Neal
Carolina Panthers

Brian was originally drafted by the Eagles out of Penn State in 1994. He was then drafted by the Carolina Panthers in the team's expansion draft in 1995. Brian is known as a solid inside runner and a good blocking back.

Mike Bedosky
Cleveland Browns

Mike was Mr. Everything coming out of the University of Missouri. He originally signed with the Atlanta Falcons and joined the Browns at the start of the 1994 season. The scouting report on Mike is that he's an extremely dedicated and hard worker and one of the brightest young players in the game. He is seen here with his wife, Ashley.

Mike Bedosky's
Hot Chicken Sandwich

Mike learned this recipe from his wife, Ashley, and his mother, Deedie.

Roster

1 loaf white bread
1 large box Velveeta™ cheese
4 cups milk
8 chicken breasts
6 eggs or 3 egg beaters
Dash salt and pepper

Game Plan

1. Line bottom of 9x13" baking dish with white bread, crusts removed.
2. Grill chicken breast and cut it into 1 inch cubes.
3. Top bread with bite size pieces of cooked chicken breast.
4. Add a layer of Velveeta cheese.
5. Top with another layer of bread.
6. Mix eggs, milk, salt and pepper together in a mixing bowl.
7. Pour mixture over casserole, cover with foil and refrigerate overnight.
8. Bake uncovered at 350 degrees for about 1 hour — bread should be golden brown.
9. Cool for 30 minutes and cut into 3x3" squares.

Serves 6

For special occasions: Combine 1 can of cream of mushroom soup with ¼ cup of cooking sherry wine. Heat and spoon over each sandwich.

Franco Harris
Pittsburgh Steelers

Franco lead the Steelers to four Super Bowl wins in his career which spanned from 1972 to 1983. He was named the MVP of Super Bowl IX for his 158 yards against the Vikings. Franco also rushed for over 1,000 yards eight times including a string of six straight seasons. He was enshrined in the Pro Football Hall of Fame in 1990. Franco is pictured above with his son, Dok.

Franco's Favorite
Baked Lasagna

Roster

3 large cloves garlic, minced
1 can tomato puree (1 lb. 13 oz.)
1 can (6 oz.) tomato paste plus 1 can water
¼ cup basil
2 tsp. salt
1 lb. lasagna noodles uncooked

8 oz. mozzarella cheese
1 lb. ground round steak
1 large onion
½ tsp. oregano
¼ cup red wine
½ cup fresh Romano cheese
1 lb. ricotta cheese

Game Plan

1. Preheat oven to 350 degrees. Lightly grease 9x13" pan.
2. Brown garlic in large skillet with ground meat. Drain any excess grease.
3. Combine onion and puree in blender until smooth, then add to meat.
4. Add all other ingredients except noodles and cheeses. Cover and simmer 10 minutes.
5. To build lasagna: Cover bottom of pan with 1/3 meat mixture.
   Grate Romano cheese over this.
   Place one layer of uncooked noodles over top.
   Spread half of the ricotta cheese evenly over noodles, then grate 4 oz. mozzarella over this.
6. Repeat, ending with meat sauce and Romano.
7. Cover tightly with foil, bake 1 hour.
8. Remove foil and let stand for about 20 minutes before serving.

Serves 6-8

This is a favorite of Franco's, his son Dok and of Franco's Italian Army!

Doug Williams

Washington Redskins

Doug is best known for his incredible performance in Super Bowl XXII against the Denver Broncos. In that game, Doug threw four touchdown passes in the second quarter alone, and hit on 18 of 29 passes for 340 yards. That day was good enough to earn him the Super Bowl MVP award and a trip to the Pro Bowl.

Doug Williams'
Red Beans and Rice

Roster

2 lb. red kidney beans
2½ lb. smoked sausage kielbasa
1 large ham hock, smoked
2 sticks celery
1 bulb garlic

1 large onion
4 qt. water
1 green bell pepper
Salt and pepper to taste

Game Plan

1. Wash beans by soaking in cold water for 30 minutes, rinse.
2. Combine all ingredients except sausage.
3. Simmer for 1½ hours, then add sausage.
4. Continue cooking until beans are tender and creamy — about 45-60 minutes longer.
5. Serve hot over white fluffy rice.

Serves 8

Swordfish au Beume Blanc à la Nick

Nick fished this recipe from the pond of Pierre Franey.

Roster

4 swordfish steaks (¾-1" thick)
2 sticks butter
1 cup white wine
Paul Prudhomme's Cajun Spice™
¾ lb. scallions
Olive oil

Game Plan

1. Brush each side of fish lightly with oil.
2. Sprinkle cajun spice on each side.
3. Heat broiler.
4. In small saucepan, combine butter and scallions, then wine.
5. Boil until mixture is reduced to ½ cup. Pour over swordfish.
6. Broil swordfish for 5-7 minutes on each side.
7. Serve with new potatoes and steamed broccoli.

Serves 4

Get a KICK out of Swordfish à la Nick!

Nick Lowery
New York Jets

One of the all time best kickers in the NFL, Nick enters the 1995 season as the leading active kicker in career field goals (349), extra points (512) and total points (1,559). Prior to joining the Jets, Nick spent 13 seasons with the Chiefs and one with the Patriots.

Classic Childress Spaghetti Sauce
Ray's wife Kara has mastered this recipe!

Roster

½ cup onion, finely chopped
1 tsp. garlic, minced
1 tsp. celery, chopped small
1 tsp. chopped parsley
½ cup olive oil

2 cups canned tomatoes
2 cups tomato puree
⅛ tsp. paprika
¼ cup sherry
Salt and pepper to taste

Game Plan

1. Sauté onion, garlic, celery and parsley in olive oil until onion and celery are soft.
2. Add tomatoes, puree and paprika.
3. Cook until well blended and thick. Season with salt and pepper.
4. Add sherry and serve at once.
5. Serve over a bed of pasta with grated Parmesan cheese on the side.

Makes 4 cups

I always eat pasta at home before gameday. They say your Friday night meal is what you play on for a Sunday noon game — so this is a weekly ritual. (High in carbohydrates and not too heavy.) I could actually eat this every night of the week because it is my favorite all-time meal.

Ray Childress
Houston Oilers

Ray is one of the premier defensive linemen in the NFL and has earned his way to five Pro Bowls. Entering 1995 Ray has 74½ career sacks. He and his wife, Kara have established the Childress Foundation to provide young people opportunities through grants and leadership awards.

Erik McMillan's
Oxtails and Rice

Roster

1 lb. oxtails
1 cup flour
1 tsp. pepper
1 Stoch Bonot pepper
1 scallion
1 clove garlic
1 tsp. Mrs. Dash™
1 tbsp. Pick-a-Pepper™ sauce
1 pkg. lima beans
1 tsp. salt

Pinch thyme
2 cups cooked white rice
1 large onion — diced
1 tsp. paprika
1 tsp. seasoned salt
3 tbsp. soy sauce — very important

Dumplings (a.k.a. Spinners):

1 cup flour
1 tsp. salt
Water

Game Plan

1. Trim all the fat from oxtails and fry or broil for 30 minutes.
2. Place in a larger pot and add salt, pepper, onions, garlic, scallion, seasoned salt, Mrs. Dash, paprika, pick-a-pepper.
3. Fill pot with water until it just covers oxtails.
4. Simmer for 1½ hours then add lima beans and soy sauce. Simmer until lima beans are tender, about 45 minutes.

Dumpling preparation:

1. Place flour and salt in bowl, adding water until it forms a paste.
2. Roll a teaspoon at a time in your hands, forming a dumpling.
3. Do this until mix is finished. Drop into the liquid in the pot of oxtails. When dumplings are done, they will float to the top.
4. Serve entire mixture over rice. Enjoy.

Serves 4

Erik McMillan
New York Jets

Erik lead the AFC in interceptions in his rookie season has been named to two Pro Bowls. He has also played for the Eagles, Browns and Chiefs.

Art Donovan's Famous Meatloaf

Roster

Meatloaf:
1 lb. lean ground beef
½ lb. ground veal
½ lb. ground pork
¾ cup chopped green pepper
¾ cup uncooked regular oats
1 large egg, beaten
1 tsp. chili powder
1 tsp. thyme

½ tsp. salt
1 tbsp. basil
2 tbsp. ketchup
¼ tsp. black pepper

Tomato gravy:
¾ cup chopped onion
2 tbsp. vegetable oil
1 tbsp. chili powder
½ tsp. salt

¼ tsp. pepper
¾ cup chopped green pepper
1 can (20 oz.) whole tomatoes, chopped and undrained
1 tbsp. basil
1 tbsp. sugar
1 tbsp. flour

Game Plan

Gravy:

1. Cook onion and pepper in oil over medium heat stirring constantly.
2. Add flour and stir until smooth.
3. Add tomatoes and other ingredients, bring to a boil.
4. Cook 5 minutes, remove from heat, and pour over meatloaf.

Meatloaf:

1. Combine all meatloaf ingredients and mix well with hands — shape into loaf.
2. Pour tomato gravy over meatloaf and bake at 350 degrees for 1½ hours.

Serves 8-10

Art Donovan
Baltimore Colts

Art's career spanned 12 seasons, eleven with the Baltimore Colts and one with the Dallas Texans. He was named to the Pro Bowl six times and he was elected into the Pro Football Hall of Fame in 1968. Considered one of the most colorful players to ever play the game, Art can be seen on numerous NFL Films episodes and has appeared on the David Letterman Show. Art is featured on the cover of this book!

Tunch Ilkin
Green Bay Packers

Tunch (pronounced TOONCH) is a native of Istanbul, Turkey. His name is as unique as his play. Prior to joining the Pack, he was selected for two Pro Bowls as a member of the Pittsburgh Steelers. Tunch is currently doing color commentary for NFL games as a member of the NBC team.

Tunch Ilkin's Chicken Cordon Bleu

Roster

2 large chicken breast halves, skinless and boneless
Salt and pepper to taste
2 thin slices boiled or baked ham
2 thin slices Swiss cheese

1 egg, beaten
$^1/_3$ cup crushed Total cereal
$^1/_4$ cup butter
1 tbsp. lemon juice
1 tbsp. white wine

Game Plan

1. Sandwich chicken between two sheets of plastic wrap and pound until cutlets are $^1/_4$ inch thick. This tenderizes them.
2. Salt and pepper to taste.
3. Put ham and cheese on top and roll up like a jelly roll. Secure with a toothpick.
4. Dip into egg, then cereal crumbs, pressing them to make them stick.
5. Brown rolls slowly in butter on all sides until chicken is cooked. (20-25 minutes)
6. Remove cutlets, add lemon juice and wine in pan juices.
7. Boil and scrape all the brown bits, pouring over the chicken cutlets.

Serves 2

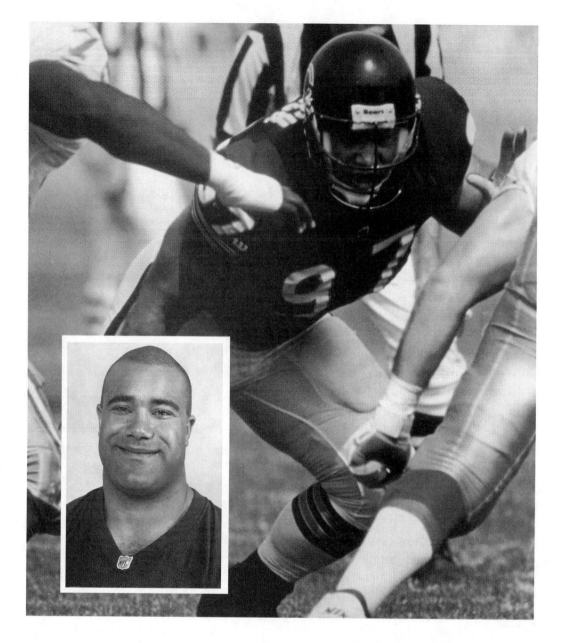

Chris Zorich

Chicago Bears

Chris is the consummate professional athlete. Not only does his hard work and ability stand out on the field, Chris is also actively and aggressively involved in a number of civic causes. The 1995 recipient of the national Henry B. Iba Citizen Athlete Award, Chris has also started the Christopher Zorich Foundation which raises money and provides services to people in need. In addition, Chris started the annual "Love Grows Here" Mother's Day event in Chicago where he delivers flowers to over 400 moms in 14 area shelters. Chris can be seen "in the kitchen" on the cover of this book!

Aunt Helen's Great
Game Day Chicken

Chris' Aunt Helen in Wisconsin has made this a game day ritual for years!

Roster

Chicken:
2 lb. boneless chicken breast with skin
2 cups soft bread crumbs (4-5 slices)
½ cup grated cheese
¼ cup melted butter
10 oz. pkg. frozen mixed vegetables

Cheese sauce:
¼ cup flour
¼ cup butter
1 cup American cheese (5-6 slices)
1 cup milk
1 cup saved broth (from chicken)
¾ tbsp. salt
¼ tbsp. pepper

Game Plan

1. Preheat oven to 350 degrees.
2. Place chicken in large skillet with enough water to cover. Boil for 10-15 minutes. Save liquid.
3. Cut chicken into bite size pieces and set aside.
4. Prepare cheese sauce. Mix all ingredients together in saucepan and cook until cheese melts.
5. Toss bread crumbs, butter, and cheese together. Save ½ cup for topping.
6. Spoon bread crumb mixture (except ½ cup) onto bottom of 2 quart casserole dish.
7. Top with vegetables, chicken, cheese sauce, and remaining bread crumbs.
8. Bake for 15 minutes, covered. Uncover and bake 10-15 additional minutes until bubbly.

Serves 6-8

My Aunt Helen serves this every Sunday the Bears play.

Roman Gabriel
L.A. Rams

Roman quarterbacked the Rams from 1962 through 1972 and holds the team record for touchdown passes with 157. He was named to four Pro Bowls and was the NFL Most Valuable Player in 1969. He finished his playing career with four solid seasons for the Eagles, earning the NFL Comeback Player of the Year award in 1973.

Roman Gabriel's Lasagna

Roster

8 oz. lasagna noodles
10 oz. part skim ricotta cheese
1 lb. ground beef
2 tbsp. olive oil
1 medium onion

32 oz. favorite tomato sauce
8 oz. cheddar cheese, grated
8 oz. mozzarella cheese, grated
Parmesan cheese, grated

Game Plan

1. Preheat oven to 350 degrees.
2. Boil noodles until slightly firm.
3. Brown beef with onion in olive oil.
4. Layer in a 13x9" lasagna pan as follows:
   1 layer noodles
   Ricotta cheese
   Meat
   Sauce
   Mixture of grated cheeses
4. Repeat, finishing with the grated cheese.
5. Sprinkle with Parmesan cheese.
6. Bake for ½ hour or refrigerate and bake later.

Serves 6-8

My wife sometimes doubles or triples this recipe and freezes lasagna for later use.

E.J. Junior III
Seattle Seahawks

E.J. was a first round draft pick by the St. Louis Cardinals in 1981 following an all-American career at Alabama. He played in two Pro Bowls as a member of the Miami Dolphins before joining the Seahawks.

Junior's Shrimp Creole

Roster

1 lb. jumbo shrimp, peeled and de-
veined
6 oz. can tomato paste
1 cup red onions, diced
1 green bell pepper, diced
2 Andoulle sausages, sliced thin

15 oz. tomato sauce
8 oz. mushrooms
3 cups okra
1 small jalapeno pepper, diced
2 cups cooked rice

Game Plan

1. Simmer all ingredients except shrimp for 25 minutes.
2. Add shrimp, simmer 5 minutes.
3. Serve over rice.

Serves 2

Alex Karras
Detroit Lions

Alex was a four time all-American at Iowa prior to becoming the first selection of the Lions in 1958 and being named to the Pro Bowl seven times. Alex starred in and produced the hit sitcom "Webster," was Howard Cosell's color man on Monday Night Football for three seasons and appeared on The Tonight Show with Johnny Carson over 20 times.

Mastaciolli à la Karras

Roster

¹/₈ lb. butter
1 jigger vodka
1 lb. mastaciolli noodles
4 tbsp. strained tomatoes
½ cup heavy cream
Grated Parmesan or Romano cheese

Game Plan

1. Cook noodles until desired tenderness.
2. Melt butter over medium heat in large sauté pan.
3. Add tomatoes and vodka, slowly stir in heavy cream.
4. Add noodles to heated mixture and simmer 5 minutes.
5. Sprinkle with grated cheese and serve immediately.

Serves 4-6

Joe Jacoby
Washington Redskins

At 6'7" and 315 pounds, Joe was an original member of the famed "Hogs" offensive line for the Redskins. Joe was also a member of four Super Bowl teams and named to four Pro Bowls.

The Famous Jacoby Baked Spaghetti

A Jacoby Family recipe

Roster

1½ lb. ground beef
30 oz. tomato sauce
6 oz. cooked spaghetti
8 oz. cream cheese
¼ cup milk
2 tbsp. butter
1 can darkest french fried onions

1 small chopped green bell pepper
1 small chopped onion
Pinch garlic powder
Salt & pepper to taste
Grated Parmesan cheese
Pinch oregano

Game Plan

1. Brown beef and season with garlic powder, oregano, salt and pepper.
2. Add spaghetti sauce and combine ½ of sauce mixture to cooked spaghetti. Set aside.
3. Sauté green peppers and onions in butter.
4. Add cream cheese and milk, blend.
5. Place spaghetti mixture in baking dish, top with cream cheese mixture, and pour remaining sauce and meat on top.
6. Sprinkle with Parmesan cheese.
7. Bake at 350 degrees for 25 minutes. Top with french fried onions, bake another 5 minutes.

Serves 6-8

This dish freezes well.

Bobby Hebert
Atlanta Falcons

Bobby was named to the Pro Bowl in 1993 in his first season as a Falcon. He began his career with a pair of USFL championship games as the leader of the Michigan Panthers and Oakland Invaders and moved on to play for the New Orleans Saints prior to joining the Falcons.

Bobby Hebert's Cajun Shrimp Fettucini

Roster

½ cup butter
¼ cup white wine
1 lb. fettucini
¼ cup finely chopped parsley
1 cup grated Parmesan cheese

$^1/_8$ tsp. black pepper
1 bunch scallions, thinly sliced
4 cloves garlic
1 lb. raw shrimp
½ tsp. crab boil

Game Plan

1. Peel and de-vein shrimp.
2. Melt butter in a large heavy skillet.
3. Sauté scallions until limp, about 2-3 minutes.
4. Add shrimp, crab boil, black pepper and wine.
5. Simmer until shrimp are just done (they will turn pink).
6. Cook fettucini until done.
7. Add fettucini to shrimp and parsley. Mix well.
8. Serve with a green salad and French bread topped with butter, garlic powder, Parmesan cheese and a sprinkle of paprika. Bon appetit!

Serves 4

Bobby grew up in Southern Louisiana and his mother and grandmother sent his wife this Cajun recipe! They continue to send her good old family Cajun recipes periodically!

Kent Hull
Buffalo Bills

Kent is a three time Pro Bowl player and he has started in four Super Bowls for the Bills. He was originally signed by the New Jersey Generals of the old USFL and he helped open holes for Hershel Walker while a member of that team. He signed with the Bills after the USFL folded in 1986 and has never left.

Hull Cabbage Casserole

This recipe came from Mawmaw (Kent's grandmother).

Roster

1 head cabbage	¼ cup red peppers
¼ cup flour	¼ cup green peppers
¼ tsp. pepper	½ cup chopped onion
¼ cup butter	½ cup mayonnaise
½ tsp. salt	¾ cup shredded cheese
2 cup evaporated milk	3 tsp. chili sauce

Game Plan

1. Preheat oven to 350 degrees.
2. Cut cabbage in small wedges and cook in salted boiling water until tender.
3. Drain, place in flat baking dish, and set aside.
4. Melt butter in small saucepan. Add flour, salt and pepper.
5. Gradually stir in milk and cook over medium heat until thickened.
6. Pour sauce over cabbage and bake at 350 degrees for 20 minutes. Combine the following ingredients and pour over cabbage:
    ¼ cup each: red and green peppers
    ½ cup chopped onion
    ½ cup mayonnaise
    ¾ cup shredded cheese
    3 tsp. chili sauce
7. Return to oven and bake 20-25 minutes longer.

Serves 8

Raymond Clayborn
New England Patriots

Raymond played the first 13 years as a member of the New England Patriots secondary. He finished his career with the Browns two years later. Raymond was named to three Pro Bowls during his career and finished with 36 interceptions.

Clayborn Fajitas
Ranchero Mexicano

Roster

1 medium onion, diced
1 tomato, diced
Monterey Jack cheese
1 bell pepper, diced
Guacamole, if desired

2 lb. fajita meat — chicken, steak or
shrimp are excellent variations
12 flour tortillas
½ lb. bacon

Game Plan

1. Prepare fajita meat as desired, cooking until medium rare. Cut into squares.
2. In a skillet, cook bacon until well done and remove, leaving about 2 tbsp. fat in pan.
3. Mix in tomato and green pepper, sauté until soft.
4. Add fajitas meat and bacon.
5. Add about ¼ cup water, stirring often until fajitas are fully cooked.
6. On a hot griddle, place tortillas with 2 slices of Monterey cheese, fold and heat until cheese is melted.
7. To serve, open tortillas with melted cheese and spoon in fajita mixture and Guacamole, and fold again.

Makes 6 servings

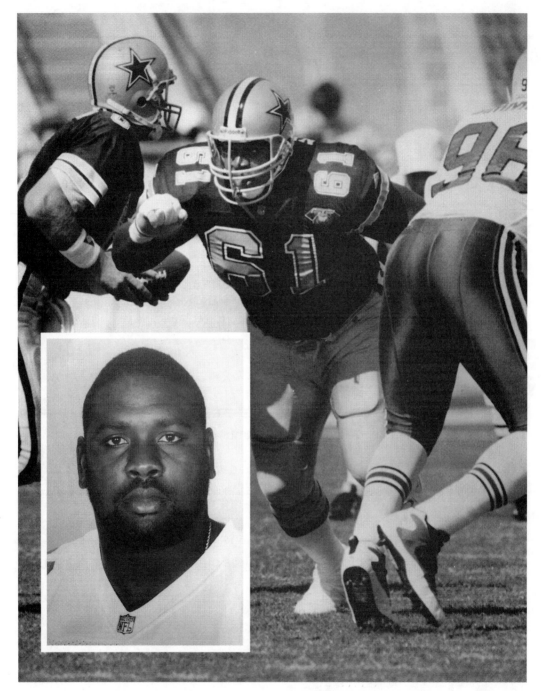

Nate Newton
Dallas Cowboys

Nate is a three time Pro Bowl performer and considered one of the top guards in the NFL. He also has been the recipient of the John Madden "Turkey Leg" award for his play on a nationally televised Thanksgiving Day game!

Nate Newton's Stuffed Lobster

Roster

2 large live lobsters

Stuffing:
½ bag Frezelles [hard Italian pepper toast]
¼ lb. scallops
¼ lb. shrimp
¼ lb. crabmeat [imitation is O.K.]
½ cup parsley
2 cloves garlic, minced
½ cup butter, melted

Game Plan

Lobsters:
1. Split each live lobster down the middle with a large, very sharp knife. Clean out cavity.
2. Remove claws and steam them until they are bright red. Remove meat from claws in one piece. Set aside.
3. Save liquid from claws.

Stuffing:
1. Soak Frezelles in claw water until soft, then squeeze.
2. Mix with all other stuffing ingredients, using hands. Mix this very well.
3. Place 2 pats of butter in each cavity, then the claw meat, then stuffing.
4. Stuff lobster from head to end of tail.
5. Bake in preheated 350 degree oven for about 30 minutes or until bright red.

Serves 2

Steve August
Seattle Seahawks

Steve was a first round draft pick of the Seahawks in the 1977 NFL draft and went on to a Pro Bowl career.

Crab & Spinach Stuffed Chicken Breasts

Roster

Sauce:
½ cup light cream
½ cup low-cal mayonnaise
2 tbsp. dried chopped onion
2 tbsp. Dijon mustard
4 tbsp. melted butter

Chicken & Stuffing:
6 large boneless, skinless chicken breasts
1 pkg. chopped frozen spinach, thawed

4 green onions, chopped
1 green pepper, chopped
4 tbsp. fresh parsley, chopped
1 cup chopped crab meat
½ cup seasoned bread crumbs
1 tbsp. Mrs. Dash™
1 cube chicken bullion
4 tbsp. butter

Game Plan

Chicken:

1. Rinse chicken and pat dry.
2. Place each breast between plastic wrap and pound with a flat-surfaced mallet to a thickness of about ¼".
3. Sprinkle each piece with salt, pepper and garlic salt.

Stuffing:

1. Preheat oven to 350 degrees.
2. Sauté onions, green pepper, parsley and spinach in butter for 5 minutes.
3. Add bullion and water, bring mixture to a boil.
4. Add crab meat, Mrs. Dash™ and bread crumbs. Turn off heat and mix.
5. Divide mixture into 6 servings.
6. Place 1 serving of stuffing in each chicken breast.
7. Roll stuffed breast to hold stuffing in.
8. Roll each stuffed breast in melted butter, then bread crumbs.
9. Set chicken rolls seam down in greased 9x13" baking pan and pour any remaining sauce over.
10. Bake in oven for about 30-35 minutes, or until meat is no longer pink and center is hot.
11. Baste and sprinkle with Parmesan cheese, then broil 4-6" below heat until cheese is browned.
12. Serve over rice.

Serves 6

Rod Milstead's San Francisco Chicken and Potatoes

This was a favorite of Rod's and his college roommate, Jason Winfield!

Roster

1 pound boneless, skinless chicken breast
or chicken breast tenders
4 medium potatoes
1 can whole kernel corn, drained

1 cup salsa
3 tbsp. virgin olive oil
2 jalapeno peppers, sliced thin
½ cup diced olives

Game Plan

1. Cut chicken into 1 inch pieces.
2. Cut potatoes into 1 inch cubes and microwave on high for 8-10 minutes.
3. Brown the chicken in olive oil on medium-high heat in a large skillet for 5 minutes.
4. Toss in the microwaved potatoes and jalapenos and sauté until potatoes are golden brown.
5. Lower heat and add in the salsa, corn and olives. Cook for 10 minutes and serve!

Serves 4

Add some sourdough bread for a good complement to this meal.

Rod Milstead
San Francisco 49ers

Rod was a third round draft choice of the Dallas Cowboys in 1992 out of Delaware State. He Joined the 49ers in 1994 and earned a Super Bowl ring following a brief stint with the Cleveland Browns.

Villapiano's Eggplant à Camposano

From a little town in Italy where Phil's father grew up.

Roster

1 large eggplant
1 (16 oz.) package of mozzarella cheese
1 (32 oz.) jar of tomato sauce (your own or commercial)
Parmesan cheese

Game Plan

1. Preheat oven to 350 degrees.
2. Line cookie sheet or broiler pan with foil & brush with oil.
3. Wash eggplant, remove the skin and slice in ½ inch pieces.
4. Arrange eggplant in broiler pan, sprinkle lightly with salt, broil until brown on both sides. Just turn once during broiling.
5. Remove broiler slices and arrange in 9x13" baking dish which has a layer of tomato sauce on the bottom.
6. Cover each slice with mozzarella cheese, then another slice of eggplant, making a little sandwich.
7. Cover with another layer of tomato sauce and sprinkle with Parmesan cheese.
8. Bake for 20-25 minutes, until sauce is bubbly and cheese is melted.

Serves 6-8

Phil Villapiano
Oakland Raiders

Phil's career with the Raiders included visits to the Super Bowl and the Pro Bowl! A key member of the famed Oakland Raider teams of the 1970's, Phil played with the likes of John Matuszak, John Davidson and Ted "The Stork" Hendricks on one of the league's most feared defenses.

Keith Rucker's
Turkey Sausage Casserole

Roster

1 lb. Italian style turkey sausage
1 cup chopped onion
1 clove garlic
1 cup chopped green or red peppers

1 cup chopped celery
1 cup uncooked rice
1 can cream of mushroom soup
1 can cream of chicken soup

Game Plan

1. Preheat oven to 350 degrees.
2. Brown sausage, then add onion, garlic, peppers and celery and cook on low until tender.
3. Add rice with undiluted soups and mix well.
4. Pour in baking dish and bake for 1½ hours, stirring occasionally.

Serves 4-6

Keith Rucker
Cincinnati Bengals

At 6'4" and over 350 pounds, Keith is a force to be dealt with on the defensive line. Known as a solid, steady performer, Keith works hard at stopping the run and he gets a good upfield push. He and Alphonso Taylor (6'2"/350lbs.) were known as the Pork & Loin Duo when they teamed up for the Cardinals.

Zeno's Oven Crisp Chicken

Roster

1 cup biscuit mix (Bisquick™ is fine)
2 tsp. salt
¼ tsp. olive oil
¼ tsp. pepper
2 tsp. paprika
1 frying chicken, cut up

Game Plan

1. Preheat oven to 350 degrees.
2. Combine biscuit mix with salt, pepper and paprika, and place in a bag.
3. Shake pieces of chicken in bag, a few at a time, coating thoroughly.
4. Lay skin side down in a single layer in oiled 9x13" pan.
5. Bake for 45 minutes, then turn and bake an additional 15 minutes longer.

Serves 4-6

Lance Zeno
St. Louis Rams

Originally signed by the Dallas Cowboys, Lance spent time as a member of the Cleveland Browns, Tampa Bay Bucs and Green Bay Packers before landing in St. Louis. He is an avid weightlifter and is a personal trainer in the off seasons.

Endzone Paella

Paella, pronounced Pie-AY-a, is a favorite of Martin and his wife, Debbie!

Roster

1½ pounds boneless, skinless chicken thighs
½ pound fresh cleaned squid, sliced into rings
1½ pounds medium shrimp, rinsed
1½ pounds mussels, rinsed well
2 medium onions, chopped
2 tbsp. chopped fresh parsley
1 green, yellow and red bell pepper, diced
2 large garlic cloves, chopped finely

6-8 saffron threads
1 bay leaf
1½ cups long grain rice
3 large tomatoes, cut into quarters
2½ cups chicken broth
2 tbsp. olive oil
½ tsp. paprika
½ tsp. salt
Fresh ground pepper to taste

Game Plan

1. Heat the oil in a deep, large frying pan (or in a paella pan, if available) over medium-high heat.
2. Quickly brown the chicken and season lightly with salt and pepper. Remove from pan and set aside.
3. Toss the onion, peppers and paprika into the pan and cook until tender, adding garlic for the last one minute to season.
4. Add the tomatoes and cook for 3-5 minutes.
5. Add the broth, saffron and bay leaf and bring it to a boil.
6. Add the rice and parsley and toss in the cooked chicken, shrimp (shell on), squid and the cleaned mussels.
7. Reduce heat and simmer covered for 20-30 minutes until the rice is cooked and the liquid evaporates.

Martin Harrison
Minnesota Vikings

Martin began his career with the San Francisco 49ers in 1990 and played there through 1993 when he had six quarterback sacks before moving on to the Vikings. He made the switch from linebacker to defensive end for the purple crew. Martin and his wife, Debbie, are active in children's charities in both the Bay Area and in the Twin Cities.

Trumbull's Scrod Mediterranean

This is a shoreline specialty of Paulette and Tony Monaco.

Roster

3 lb. very thick scrod or cod fish (you may double up on thin slices if necessary)

Sauce:
1 large can Italian tomatoes (whole or chunks)
4 large cloves garlic

$^1/_3$ cup pitted Greek olives, sliced
4-6 anchovies (or more to taste)
Fresh parsley
Fresh basil
Salt and pepper to taste
$^1/_4$ cup capers
Olive oil

Game Plan

1. Sauté garlic in 3 tbsp. olive oil until lightly browned.
2. Add all other sauce ingredients and cook over low-medium heat for about 20 minutes.
3. Place fish flat on bottom of lasagna pan.
4. Pour sauce over fish and bake, uncovered, for about 15-20 minutes at 400 degrees
5. Fish is done when it is bubbly and flakes.
6. Sprinkle grated Italian cheese over top just before serving.

Serves 6-8

This meal is outstanding when served over angel hair pasta.

Rick Trumbull
Tampa Bay Buccaneers

Rick began his career as an offensive tackle with the Bengals and moved on to the Cleveland Browns before Tampa Bay traded for him in 1994.

John Hannah
New England Patriots

John was tabbed the "Greatest Offensive Lineman Ever" by Sports Illustrated *and was named to nine Pro Bowls during his career. Born in Canton, Georgia, he was inducted into the Pro Football Hall of Fame in Canton, Ohio in 1991.*

Aunt Mary's Chicken Salad

John learned this recipe from his wife Page's Aunt Mary Henry.

Roster

8 chicken breasts
2 onions, sliced
3 celery tops
2 tbsp. lemon juice
¾ cup chopped celery

½ to 1 cup mayonnaise
4 oz. sour cream
½ cup toasted almonds
½ cup pineapple
Salt and pepper to taste

Game Plan

1. Combine chicken, onions, and celery tops and bake at 375 degrees for 25 minutes.
2. Remove from heat and cool.
3. Cut up chicken and marinate it in lemon juice and sour cream overnight.
4. Combine almonds, chopped celery, and pineapple with chicken. Salt and pepper to taste.
5. Finally, mix in mayonnaise, starting with ½ cup.
6. Mix and serve.

Serves 8

James Williams
New York Giants

James is a man of many nicknames on the field, including J-Dub, Dog, Deuce-Deuce and the Silent Assassin. He spent time with both the Oilers and Colts before landing in the Big Apple. The word on James is that he's quicker than a hiccup! James is pictured above with the owner of Guliana's restaraunt in Edinboro, Scotland.

Shrimp For Hire!

Roster

15 jumbo shrimp (peeled and de-veined)
1 can of cream of shrimp soup
1 small can of evaporated milk
1 small onion, diced
1 bell pepper, diced
1 green onion, diced
1 very large onion sliced thin
½ stick unsalted butter
2 tbsp. Cajun seasoning
2 cups of prepared cooked rice

Game Plan

1. Melt butter in sauté pan on medium heat.
2. Add chopped onion, pepper and mushroom and sauté for 2 minutes.
3. Toss shrimp with Cajun seasoning and add to the sauté pan for 2 minutes.
4. Add cream of shrimp soup and evaporated milk.
5. Simmer until reduced by about half.
6. Serve over rice and sprinkle the diced green onion on top.

Serves 4

Note: You may substitute lobster bisque for cream of shrimp soup!

Kinnebrew Scallop Supreme

Roster

1 lb. fresh bay scallops
½ tsp. salt
½ cup white wine
3 tbsp. butter
½ lb. sliced mushrooms
1 cup sliced green onions

3 tbsp. flour
½ cup water
1¼ cup light cream
1 tbsp. lemon juice
2 tbsp. chopped pimento
Dash pepper

Topping: 1 cup soft bread crumbs mixed with 1 tbsp. melted butter

Game Plan

1. Preheat oven to 400 degrees.
2. Simmer scallops in water, wine and salt until tender (about 5 min. max.)
3. Save liquid, reduce it to ¾ cup.
4. Sauté mushrooms in butter until tender. Add celery and green onions, cook 3 minutes.
5. Stir in flour, salt and pepper, add cream and scallop liquid. Simmer until thickened.
6. Add lemon juice, scallops and pimento and stir gently.
7. Place in scalloped baking shells or a glass baking dish and top with bread crumbs.
8. Bake for 10-12 minutes.

Serves 6

Larry Kinnebrew
Cincinnati Bengals

Larry was one of the biggest fullbacks in the NFL during his career with the Bengals and a go-to man in short yardage situations.

Banana Split

Desserts

Overtime
Scorecard

Orange Juice Cake

Lomas' wife Dolores tackles this recipe on special occasions!

Roster

3 cups sugar
3 cups flour
8 eggs
½ cup orange juice

4 sticks butter
1 tsp. vanilla extract
1 tsp. lemon extract

Game Plan

1. Preheat oven to 350 degrees.
2. In a mixing bowl, *cream sugar and butter until thoroughly blended.
3. Add eggs one at a time until each is blended.
4. Slowly add 1 cup of flour at a time.
5. Blend in vanilla and lemon extracts, and lastly, the orange juice.
6. Bake in greased and lightly floured 9x9" pan for 1½ hours or until done.

Serves 8

* the term "cream" means to blend together as one.

Lomas Brown
Detroit Lions

Lomas has been the main man opening holes for Barry Sanders and has been named to four straight Pro Bowls entering 1995. Lomas and his wife have an annual Lomas Brown Foundation dinner to assist the Detroit Big Brothers/Big Sisters program in raising scholarship money for underprivileged children in need.

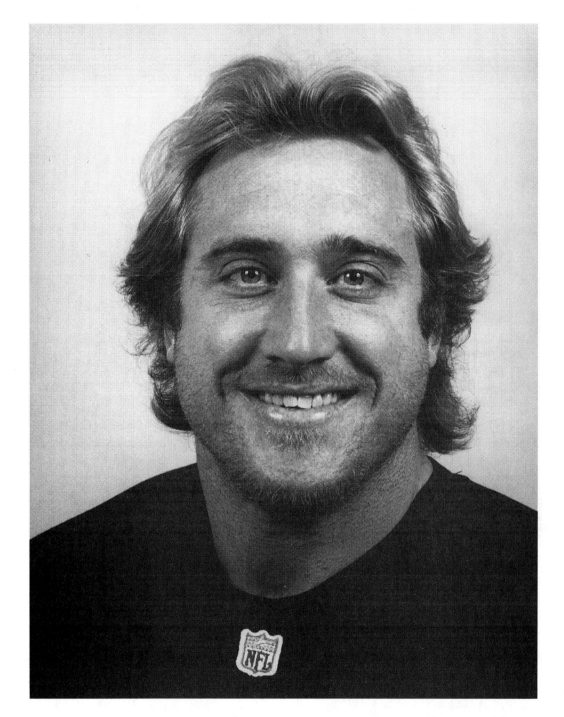

Kevin Greene
Pittsburgh Steelers

Kevin is an animated and emotional player who has a reputation for playing in a wild frenzy to get to the quarterback. Kevin is closing in on 100 career sacks and has been named to two Pro Bowls.

Greene's Patented Protein Shake

Roster

2 whole eggs
20 oz. whole milk
2 bananas
8 oz. pineapple or orange juice
3 heaping tablespoons high protein powder

Game Plan

Blend and drink!

Excellent for a pick-me-up and a high protein blast!

Russ Grim
Washington Redskins

Russ was a fixture on the offensive line for the Redskins for 11 seasons, including three Super Bowls and a Pro Bowl appearance.

Grim's Great Banana
Split Dessert

Roster

2 cups graham cracker crumbs
½ cup margarine
½ cup chopped walnuts
1 cup pitted bing cherries
1 can crushed pineapple, drained

½ cup sugar
¼ tsp. cinnamon
1 large pkg. banana pudding
3 bananas, sliced
1 container cool whip

Game Plan

1. Mix the graham cracker crumbs, sugar, margarine and cinnamon together and press into 9x13" pan, use as pie crust.
2. Prepare pudding according to directions, let cool.
3. Mix pudding, sliced bananas, drained pineapple and cool whip.
4. Pour into pie crust.
5. Top with nuts and cherries.
6. Refrigerate for 4 hours before serving.

Serves 8

James Parrish

Pittsburgh Steelers

At 6'6" and over 320 pounds, James has the natural ability to become one of the League's top offensive linemen. He earned his first Super Bowl ring as a member of the Dallas Cowboys squad in 1993. James enjoyed stints with the Dolphins, Chargers, 49ers, Colts and Cowboys before settling in with the Steelers. He is also fluent in Japanese!

Maria's Parfait Cake

James negotiated this recipe from his agent's wife, Maria Sheehy!

Roster

6 Skor™ candy bars, frozen and broken into tiny pieces
1 chocolate cake (store bought is fine — no frosting)
3 medium cartons Cool Whip Lite™
1 attractive see-through glass bowl

Game Plan

Divide everything into thirds for three layers
1. Break cake into small cubes and layer on bottom of bowl.
2. Layer Cool Whip™ over the cake cubes.
3. Add a layer of Skor pieces over Cool Whip™.
4. Continue layering — ending with Cool Whip™.
5. Sprinkle with chocolate shots or more crushed Skor™ candy.
6. Keep refrigerated until ready to serve — best if refrigerated for at least two hours.

Serves 8

This dessert is absolutely delicious and is always a big hit.

Bobby Grier
New England Patriots

Bobby is the Director of Player Personnel and a main reason for the resurgence of the Patriots. His son Mike is an all-American hockey player from Boston University and a draft pick of the St. Louis Blues.

Bobby Grier's Pumpkin Cheesecake

Roster

1 pkg. spice cake mix
3 (8 oz.) pkg. softened cream cheese
1 can pumpkin
1 tbsp. pumpkin pie spice
½ cup sugar

2 cups whipping cream, chilled
½ cup melted butter
4 eggs
1 (14 oz.) can sweetened condensed milk
1(2½ oz.) sliced almonds

Game Plan

For crust:

1. Combine cake mix with melted butter and press into bottom of ungreased springform pan.

For filling:

1. Combine cream cheese with condensed milk in a large bowl & beat with electric mixer for about 2 minutes.
2. Add pumpkin, eggs and spices, and continue beating on high for 1 minute.
3. Pour over prepared crust and bake in preheated 375 degree oven for 65 minutes or until set.
4. Cool completely on rack. Refrigerate 2 hours.
5. Loosen cake from sides of pan. Remove sides of pan.

For topping:

1. Preheat oven to 300 degrees.
2. Toast almonds on baking sheet for 4-5 minutes until golden brown.
3. Cool completely.
4. Beat whipping cream until soft peaks form. Gradually add sugar — beat until stiff.
5. Spread over top of chilled cake, garnish with toasted almonds.
6. Refrigerate until ready to serve.

Serves 8-10

Sam Wyche

Tampa Bay Buccaneers

Sam is one of the most respected head coaches in the NFL with management and players alike. A former quarterback in the NFL with Cincinnati, Buffalo, St. Louis and Washington, Sam has been to the Super Bowl as both a player and head coach.

Wyche's Key Lime Pie

Roster

1 can Eagle Brand™ condensed milk
1 medium size carton Cool Whip™
½ can frozen lime juice, thawed
1 ready made graham cracker crust
3-4 drops green food coloring

Game Plan

1. Blend all ingredients except Cool Whip™, pour into pie shell and chill overnight.
2. Top with Cool Whip™ before serving.

Serves 8

Note: For crispier crusts, beat an egg and brush on crust. Bake at 400 degrees for five minutes.

Hoby Brenner
New Orleans Saints

Entering the 1995 season, Hoby has played his entire 15 year career with the New Orleans Saints. He was named to the Pro Bowl in 1987.

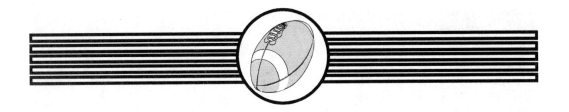

Paper Bag Apple Pie

Hoby was jazzed to get this recipe from Gloria Davis.

Roster

1 unbaked 9" pie shell
½ cup sugar
½ tsp. nutmeg
2 tbsp. lemon juice
4 large baking apples, peeled and sliced
into ½ inch thick pieces

2 tbsp. flour
½ tsp. cinnamon
1 heavy brown paper bag

Game Plan

1. Mix all ingredients, pour into pie shell.
2. Place pie in heavy brown bag and fold end over. Fasten with paperclips.
3. Place bag in preheated 425 degree oven for 1 hour.
4. Cut bag open and cool pie.

Serves 8

Note: Use a recycled bag so it won't burn.

Bob Lilly
Dallas Cowboys

Bob played with the Cowboys and terrorized opposing quarterbacks for 14 years beginning in 1961 and was named to the Pro Bowl seven times. He was inducted into the Hall of Fame in 1980.

Punchbowl Cake

Bob learned this recipe from his Aunt Ree Lilly.

Roster

1 small angel food cake
1 large can crushed pineapple
1 large carton Cool Whip™

1 large pkg. instant vanilla pudding
Milk for pudding
1 can cherry pie filling

Game Plan

1. Break ½ of angel food cake into chunks and put on bottom of punchbowl.
2. Drain pineapple, layer on top of cake.
3. Mix vanilla pudding as directed, layer over pineapple.
4. Layer remaining cake over pudding.
5. Next, top with cherry pie filling.
6. Top with Cool Whip™ and refrigerate.

Serves 8-10

You may decorate with coconut, pecans or sprinkle colored shots over top.

Louis DeFilippo
New York Giants

Big Lou played with the Giants during the 1940's following an honor-filled career at Fordham. He went on to become a legendary coach at Derby (CT) High School where he inspired and influenced the lives of hundreds of players.

DeFilippo's Carrot Cake

This recipe is a favorite of Lou's wife, Dolly.

Roster

Cake:
3 eggs, beaten
2 cups sugar
1⅓ cups oil
2 cups flour
1 tsp. baking powder
2 tsp. cinnamon
1 tsp. salt
1 tsp. vanilla
2 cups grated carrots

1 cup chopped walnuts
1 8 oz. can crushed pineapple
1 cup flaked coconut

Frosting:
1 6 oz. package cream cheese
1½ cups confectionery sugar
1 tsp. vanilla
1tsp. water

Game Plan

1. Preheat oven to 350 degrees
2. Combine eggs, sugar, oil, vanilla and dry ingredients.
3. Stir in carrots, pineapple, nuts and coconut.
4. Bake 45-50 minutes in 9x13" pan or tube pan

Frosting:

1. Blend all ingredients until smooth and spreadable. You may add water if necessary for proper consistency.
2. Spread on cooled cake.

Serves 12

Louis Riddick
Cleveland Browns

Louis is a former Thorpe Award Finalist, provost scholar and deans list student out of the University of Pittsburgh. He began his career with the 49ers and moved on to the Falcons before settling in as a top performer in the NFL for the Cleveland Browns. Louis is the founder of the Hit The Books pro-education campaign.

Pineapple Cream Cake

Roster

Cake:
2 cups sugar
2 cups flour
2 eggs
1 cup nuts
2 tsp. baking soda
1 tsp. vanilla
1 can crushed pineapple 16 oz.
   (undrained)

Icing:
¾ stick of butter
8 oz. cream cheese
1⅓ cup confectioners sugar
1 tsp. vanilla
1 cup crushed walnuts or almonds

Game Plan

1. Preheat oven to 350 degrees.
2. Beat all cake ingredients until well mixed.
3. Bake in a 9x13" glass pan for 45 minutes or until center is set.

Icing:

1. Beat all ingredients together until spreadable and spread over a luke warm cake.
2. Sprinkle with nuts.

Serves 10

Ricotta Cake

This is a favorite of Frank's fans Carol and George Geanuracous.

Roster
1 package yellow cake mix
3 lb. ricotta cheese
8 eggs
1 tsp. vanilla

Game Plan
1. Preheat oven to 350 degrees.
2. Mix cake mix according to directions and pour into 9x13" baking pan.
3. Mix remaining ingredients well and pour over top of cake mixture, being careful not to mix the two layers.
4. Bake for 1 hour.
5. Shut oven off but keep cake in oven for an additional hour.

Serves 10

This cake is the best!

Frank Giannetti
Indianapolis Colts

Frank played both linebacker and defensive tackle for the Colts for two seasons after a super Penn State career. He also spent 1994 on injured reserve with the Falcons as he tore a bicep muscle while sacking quarterback Steve DeBerg.

Undra's Graham Cracker Cake and Vanilla Cream Frosting

Roster

Cake:
1 cup flour
1 heaping cup sugar
3½ tsp. baking powder
¾ tsp. salt
¾ cup shortening
2 cups crushed graham crackers
1 cup + 2 tbsp. milk

1½ tsp. vanilla
2 eggs, beaten

Frosting
½ cup butter
3½ cup sifted confectioner's sugar
5 tbsp. light cream
1 tsp. vanilla extract

Game Plan

1. Preheat oven to 375 degrees.
2. Mix all dry ingredients together well until blended.
3. Add shortening and mix well. This will make a lumpy mixture.
4. Fold in milk, vanilla and eggs. Beat with electric mixer for about 3 minutes.
5. Pour the entire mixture into a greased and floured 9x13" cake pan.
6. Bake for 30-35 minutes.

Frosting:

1. Lightly brown butter in small skillet over low heat. Remove from heat.
2. Combine butter, sugar, light cream and vanilla in medium mixing bowl.
3. Beat with an electric mixer until mixture is smooth and fluffy.
4. Spread evenly over cake!

Serves 10

Undra Johnson
Dallas Cowboys

Undra began his career with the Falcons following an 11-1 season with the West Virginia Mountaineers. He also played for the New Orleans Saints and the San Antonio Riders of the World League before joining the Cowboys.

Curt Warner
Seattle Seahawks

Curt was a first round selection of the Seahawks in the 1983 NFL draft and enjoyed a spectacular career. He led the NFL in rushing TDs and carries as a rookie and lead the AFC in rushing yards his rookie season and again in 1986. Curt was named to several Pro Bowl squads.

Macadamia Nut Pie

This recipe is a specialty of Curt's housekeeper, Paula Farrell.

Roster

3 large eggs
$^2/_3$ cup sugar
1 cup light corn syrup
$^1/_3$ cup melted butter

$1^1/_4$ cup halved macadamia nuts
9" unbaked pie shell
Cool Whip™

Game Plan

1. Preheat oven to 350 degrees.
2. In a large mixing bowl, beat the eggs. Add the sugar, corn syrup and butter. Beat together.
3. Add the macadamia nuts and stir together.
4. Pour the mixture into the pie shell and bake for 50 minutes or until you can slice a knife in and it comes out clean.
5. Let stand for 15 minutes and top with a spoonful of Cool Whip™.

Serves 8

Chef Leo's Cream Cheese Cake Flavored with Liqueur

An irresistable dessert created by Chef Leo, served at Leo Sr. and Angelina Moscato's Olde Birmingham Restaurant in Derby, Connecticut

Roster

Cake:
1 lb. cream cheese
1 pt. heavy cream
1 cup granulated sugar
2 large whole eggs and 1 egg yolk
2 oz. Grand Marnier Liqueur
1 oz. fresh lemon juice
1 tsp. vanilla abstract
1 tsp. salt

Topping:
16 oz. sour cream

Crust:
8 oz. ginger snap crumbs
3 tbsp. melted butter

Game Plan

1. Preheat the oven to 300 degrees.
2. Topping: in a bowl, stir sour cream and let stand at room temperature until ready to use on cake.
3. Crust: Mix ginger snap crumbs with melted butter and press evenly into an 8 inch spring form pan.
4. Batter: With a blender, cream sugar, egg yolk and cream cheese until thoroughly blended.
5. Add eggs to batter mix one at a time until each is thoroughly blended.
6. Add heavy cream in a slow steady stream to batter, scraping bowl with a rubber spatula as you go.
7. Add Grand Marnier Liqueur, lemon juice, vanilla and salt to cake batter, blend one more minute.
8. Pour batter into 8 inch springform pan with prepared ginger snap crust.
9. Bake for one hour and fiften minutes. Remove from oven.
10. Carefully spread sour cream over top of cake and place in oven for five minutes more. Remove cake to a cooling rack to cool.
11. Place cake in refrigerator to set overnight.

Serves 10-12

The Playbook

Our best sneaks, end-arounds, and ways to defend against a bomb!

Apples An apple a day? Sure, but what kind? Good all purpose apples are Baldwin, Granny Smith, Johnathan and Winesap apples. The best to "pick-and-eat" are Golden Delicious, McIntosh and Red Delicious, and the best for cooking are the Rhode Island, Greening, Rome Beauty and York Imperial apples.

To keep peeled apples white spray them with lemon juice immediately after you cut them.

Artichokes Do not cook artichokes in aluminum or iron pots, as they will turn the pots gray in color. Glass and stainless steel pots are recommended.

Boiling Did you know that water boils at 212 degrees?

Broccoli Peel the stalks of broccoli (the ones you usually throw away), slice them thinly and use them in soups, salads and as a great flavor to your stuffing mix.

Cauliflower Add milk to the water when cooking cauliflower as this keeps it white in color.

Capers Capers add zip to sauces, fish, chicken and veal dishes. Capers are the bud of a flower from a caper bush and are usually packed in salt or a vinegar brine.

Chicken When broiling (especially skinless), baste the chicken with white wine or lemon juice to keep it moist and to add another level of flavor to the bird.

Chocolate A microwave oven is a quick and easy way to melt chocolate. Be sure to stir it every 30 seconds to maintain proper consistency.

Cooling To quickly cool a pot of sauce, place the pot in the kitchen sink with a bath of ice and water, stirring frequently.

Corn   Do not add salt to boiling water when cooking corn as this will toughen the kernels.

Deep Frying   When deep frying, a technique where the food is completely submerged in oil, the ideal oil temperature is 375 degrees.

Dressing   As a low-fat alternative to oil, substitute with chicken stock when making salad dressing.

Eggs   When boiling eggs, place the uncooked eggs in rapidly boiling water to prevent leakage from a cracked shell. Do not put in water and wait for it to boil.

Egg whites left out at room temperature for 30 minutes will increase the volume when whipped. Be sure to use absolutely clean utensils when whipping these as well.

To separate egg whites from the yolk, crack the egg in half and flip-flop the yolk from one shell to the other allowing the whites to fall.

Fire   When a grease fire occurs, throw salt or baking soda to quickly extinguish it. Contrary to some reports, do not use flour as this may cause the fire to go out of control.

Fish   Don't bother asking if the fish is fresh. Use the "see and sniff" test with all fish. Fish should be odor free and should not have any "slime" on it at all. Whole fish should have bulging clear eyes and bright pink to red gills.

Garlic   When cooking garlic, avoid burning it or it will become very bitter.

Gravy   A small amount of brown sugar is the quick fix to a salty gravy.

Grilling   Seafood generally cooks quicker than other meat products so be sure not to over cook. Do not place seafood and meat on the grill at the same time unless you are planning to eat the fish first. Ideal grilling temperature is 540 degrees.

Lettuce   After washing lettuce, dry as much as possible so the dressing can adhere to the leaves. When wet, the dressing gets watered down and slides off the leaves.

Marinade   A liquid used to flavor and tenderize foods. Liquids usually have a high acid content, such as lemon, vinegar and most wines. Submerge foods in this liquid to create versatile flavors. Spices are also added for pungent flavors.

Molasses   To easily remove molasses and other sticky liquids from a measuring cup, spray the cup first with a vegetable oil spray.

Mushrooms   Always store mushrooms in a paper bag. This allows them to breath. Plastic bags seal in the moisture and cause the mushrooms to develop a slimy texture.

Mustard   A delightful flavor change can be added to mustard by adding fresh cracked pepper, green peppercorns, fresh herbs, roasted garlic and a variety of other ingredients. Experiment a little with the versatile condiment.

Onions   To reduce the "power" of sliced raw onions, soak them in ice cold water for about 30 minutes. This will allow for a milder flavor.

When storing onions, it is a good idea to store them in a mesh bag or in a metal wire basket for proper breathability.

Oops!   For that stray spot of BBQ sauce on your shirt, quickly rub it with cold club soda.

Ovens   Conventional ovens have stagnant heat, therefore preheating is necessary. Convection ovens utilize a fan to circulate the heat evenly around the food so preheating is usually not necessary and foods cook more quickly.

Pan Frying   The method of cooking where the food is only partially covered with oil, is excellent for larger pieces of food items. When frying, do not allow the foods to touch in the pan. This over crowding can actually cause the cooking method to change to more of a steaming method with all of the oil being soaked up in the food.

Paper   When a recipe calls for a dish to be baked in paper (en Papillote), foil can be used instead.

Pasta   When boiling water for pasta, add salt only when you add the pasta as the salt tends to leave a stale taste after prolonged boiling.

To prevent the pot of water from boiling over, add three tablespoons of oil to the water. This will also help keep the pasta from sticking to each other.

To avoid "sticky spaghetti," run fresh hot water in to the pot before draining. This will help prevent the strands bonding together.

The ideal way to cook pasta is to drop it in the water which has been brought to rapid boil. This creates an even cooking procedure.

Dried pasta, such as the packaged variety bought in most stores, can be kept indefinitely if stored in a cool, dry place.

Peppers   To roast peppers, place them directly over an open flame or broiler until charred. Then place them directly in a covered container to steam. Let cool, peel and remove the seeds.

Poaching   The ideal poaching temperature is between 170 and 180 degrees with no water movement or bubbles at all.

Potatoes   To keep peeled potatoes white, blanch them in boiling water for about two minutes. This will prevent the yellowing color which otherwise naturally occurs.

                   When storing potatoes, it is a good idea to store them in a mesh bag or in a metal wire basket for proper breathability.

Rice   For whiter rice, add lemon juice to the water when cooking.

Roasting   When roasting, use a shallow pan rather than a deep one as it allows the heat to circulate more evenly when cooking.

Saffron   Ounce for ounce the most expensive spice in the world. Packaged in powdered or string form, saffron will add a fragrant flavor in rice and soup dishes and adds a far eastern flair to any dish.

Sauté   A method of cooking in which items are quickly cooked in a very small amount of fat..usually in a sauté pan. To ensure proper color of a sautéed item, be sure it is completely dry before placing it in the pan.

Shrinkage   Meats cooked at a lower temperature for longer periods of time will retain most of their original size. Meats cooked quickly at high temperatures will experience much more shrinkage.

Simmering   Simmering method is achieved by bringing the product to a boil, then turning down the heat to proper temperature. The ideal simmering temperature is between 185 and 195 degrees, with tiny bubbles rising to the top of the liquid.

Steaming   Steaming is a method of preparing food with the food suspended above a small amount of boiling water. The vapor from the steam cooks the food. Steaming is an excellent method of cooking to retain the nutrients in vegetables. Only a small amount of water is needed to create the steaming effect.

Stir Frying   Prepare all foods for cooking before you start the stir fry process, as cooking is usually done all at once with this method. Also, cut the food all one size for quick and uniform cooking.

Stock Do not boil stock, as it will incorporate the scum and fat which will accumulate at the top and cause the stock to become cloudy and un-appetizing. Stock should be simmered slowly for proper reduction and the fat and scum should be skimmed off the top.

Stuffing Cook your stuffing "on the side" rather than in the bird. Bacteria can develop from an improperly cooked part of the bird which is insulated from the heat by the stuffing.

Temperatures Meat temperatures are a vital part of food handling and safety. As a general guideline, the internal temperature of poultry is 180 degrees; pork should be a minimum of 160 degrees, and beef and lamb is 140 degrees. Test this with a meat thermometer.

Thermometer The use of a cooking thermometer when roasting large pieces of meat will show accurate internal temperatures.

To test the accuracy of a cooking thermometer, place it in rapidly boiling water as it should read 212 degrees.

Tomatoes To peel tomatoes, blanch them in boiling water for 15 seconds, immediately cool under cold water and peel.

To enhance their flavor, add a pinch of sugar when cooking.

The best way to ripen a tomato indoors off the vine is to place it out of the sunlight at room temperature.

Utensils Use wooden utensils and avoid cooking foods with high acid content, such as tomatoes when cooking in aluminum pots. Scraping aluminum pots and pans with a metal utensil will discolor the food, especially white sauces.

Bon Appetit!